It's Your Constitution

Governing Australia Today

It's Your Constitution

Governing Australia Today

Cheryl Saunders

Director, Centre for Comparative Constitutional Studies,
University of Melbourne

The Federation Press
1998

Published in Sydney by:
    The Federation Press
    PO Box 45, Annandale, NSW, 2038.
    71 John St, Leichhardt, NSW, 2040.
    Ph (02) 9552 2200. Fax (02) 9552 1681.

National Library of Australia
Cataloguing-in-Publication entry:
    Saunders, Cheryl
    It's your Constitution: Governing Australia today

    ISBN 1 86287 244 9

    1. Constitutional law – Australia. I. Title.

342.9402

Typeset by The Federation Press, Leichhardt, NSW.
    Printed by Australian Print Group, Maryborough, Victoria.

Preface

This is an important time for Australians. On 1 January 2001, the Australian Constitution will have been in use for exactly 100 years. A public debate is under way about whether Australia should become a republic. Delegates have been elected to a Constitutional Convention to discuss this and to consider what a model for a republic might be. As the centenary comes closer, other suggestions for changing the Constitution might be raised as well.

Any changes to the Constitution must be approved by Australian voters, just as they were 100 years ago. But whether changes are made or not, the centenary is a good opportunity for Australians to find out more about their own Constitution. We live in a democracy, and need to know how our system of government works.

This book was written to explain what the Constitution is, what it says and why it matters for the way in which we govern ourselves. To make it useful for as many people as possible I have tried to use language and ideas which are familiar. The only authorities I have referred to are the main sections of the Constitution and a few of the most important High Court decisions (and even then without citations). Constitutional scholars and people who work regularly with the Constitution will find this unusual, but I hope that they will understand why I have taken this approach.

I have also tried to make the book as interesting as possible. For that purpose, it is organised around three questions, which many people ask about government. What say do I have in what goes on? Who makes government decisions, and how? What are the limits on what governments can do? Where relevant, I have drawn attention to some of the current issues for the Constitution, to assist people to understand them and, if they wish, to join in discussions about them.

The original idea for a book of this kind came from Chris Holt. He encouraged me to write it and has been extraordinarily helpful and patient ever since. He and his colleagues at Federation Press have been a pleasure to work with. My particular thanks go to Kathy Fitzhenry, for all her assistance in the final stages of production and to Carol Bois, who was a rigorous editor, from whom I learned a great deal.

My thanks also to Tracey Cromby, Administrative Assistant to the Centre for Comparative Constitutional Studies, who handled many of the logistics as time began running out, as calmly as usual. And to Ian and Hilde, who put up with a lot at home.

Cheryl Saunders
Melbourne Law School
January 1998

Contents

What is a Constitution?

There are constitutions everywhere

Suppose you want to set up a club, so that your favourite sport can be played in your area; or to provide services to your community; or just for social purposes.

You need others who are interested; a place to meet; probably, some money. But you also need a clear idea about what the club is going to do and how it is going to do it. What are its aims? Who can become a member? Who can make decisions for the club? If there is a committee, how is it chosen, and how often? Should there be anything the committee cannot do without asking the members: raising membership fees, for example, or changing club colours? Who will be responsible, if things go wrong?

These questions need to be answered in a set of basic rules for the club. When the rules are put together, they are likely to be called a "constitution" although other terms (for example, "charter") are sometimes used as well.

The constitution need not include every detail about how the club will work. The number of teams, or the hours when the club-house will be open can be decided in other ways, from time to time. Only the rules which you and the other members think are the most important should be in the constitution. If you draw them up carefully enough in the first place, you can expect them to last for quite a while.

But times change. In the future, you might want to merge with another club; or provide different services; or create a new category of members; or make the management committee bigger or smaller. So you need a procedure for changing the constitution. And because these rules provide the very basis on which the club operates, the procedure for changing them is likely to require broad agreement. In some cases, it may involve the consent of the members themselves.

All organisations have constitutions: not just sporting clubs and community groups but companies, unions and associations of every kind. And countries have constitutions too, which describe how decisions are made on behalf of the whole community.

This book is about constitutions of this kind and, in particular, about the Australian Constitution. But the underlying idea is much the same, whether you are dealing with a constitution for a country or part of a country (such as a state), or with a constitution for any other group.

What does a constitution look like?

There are nearly 200 countries in the world at present. All of them have a constitution. And almost every one of them has a single document which is called The Constitution. The United Kingdom is an exception, as we will see.

All these constitutions are different, because they have to meet the different needs of the countries concerned. But they have some things in common.

Constitutions provide only the most important rules for a community. Other rules, or "laws", can be made by other bodies (in particular, by Parliament). But these must be consistent with the Constitution.

Constitutions usually are written in general terms, because they are intended to last for a long time.

Constitutions tend to be short, in comparison with other kinds of laws. Some are very short indeed. The Constitution of Indonesia, for example, has only 37 sections. As a contrast, the new South African Constitution is much longer, with 243 sections. The South Africans wanted to give constitutional protection to more of their system of government than many other countries do. The Australian Constitution is somewhere in between, with 128 sections, and fits easily into a pocket-size edition.

The language used in constitutions is often more inspiring and straightforward than the language used in other laws. A constitution is a national symbol, like the flag or the anthem. A constitution can help to bind a community together, if people are proud of it and what it stands for. And a constitution is the most important law of all for people to understand. In a democracy, government gets its authority from the people. They need to know how government works and what it is able to do.

When did written constitutions begin?

Historically, constitutions are associated with the idea of limits on government. If a single person, or group of people, have absolute or total power to govern, there is not much point in writing a constitution to say so. Constitutions became useful when it was accepted that governments should change from time to time and that their power should be limited. A constitution provided the means for describing how the government should be chosen and what it could do. Nowadays, the usual procedure for choosing a government involves democratic elections, of one kind or another. Constitutions provide the basic rules for these elections. In this way, Constitutions have become linked with democracy as well.

The first modern constitutions were written in the United States, Poland and France in the late 1700s. Gradually, other countries acquired constitutions too. Sometimes the reason was the same: there had been a revolution which changed the system of government and a constitution was needed to provide a framework for it.

But systems of government change for other reasons as well, in ways that require a new constitution. Australia's own experience is an example of this. When the six Australian colonies decided to join together in 1901 they needed a Constitution for the new national government which this would create and to describe their own relations with it. The Australian Constitution was the result.

One country which does not have a single, constitutional document is the United Kingdom. Limited government developed gradually in that country over a long period of time, and a set of rules and practices grew up around it. Nothing has happened so far to cause those rules and practices to be brought together in a permanent written constitution. In the United Kingdom, therefore, the constitution is still made up of a variety of different sources, including key laws or "Acts" of Parliament, decisions of courts, political practices or conventions and the treaties which form the European Union.

Making and changing Constitutions

Constitutions describe the system of government. They therefore say something about how all other laws will be made. This makes constitutions more important than other laws.

How should constitutions themselves be made? The answer is: in whatever way is acceptable to the community for whom the system of government is established. These days, this usually means that the people themselves should have some say in deciding what goes into their constitution or, at least, that they should have a chance to approve it before it finally becomes law. As we will see, this happened in Australia, where the original Constitution was drafted by elected representatives and was approved by the voters in all colonies in a popular vote, or referendum.

Ordinary laws can be changed by Parliament. The procedure for changing constitutions is usually different and more difficult. This is because constitutions are supposed to last longer than other laws. In Australia, the procedure for changing the Constitution is similar to the way in which it originally was made. The Australian Constitution was approved by referendum towards the end of the 19th century and it can only be changed by referendum now.

What do you find in constitutions?

Constitutions are more important and more difficult to change than other laws. It follows that each constitution should cover those parts of the system of government which the people in that country are most anxious to protect. At the very least, this is likely to include the way in which the government is chosen, the limits on its powers and the independence of judges and courts. Constitutions of countries like Australia, which divide power between different governments such as the Commonwealth and the States, will provide the main rules for this as well.

In addition, different countries are likely to have particular concerns which they try to protect through the constitution. So, for example, the Constitution of Germany allows it to be a member of the European Union; the Constitution of Japan prohibits the use of armed force; the Constitution of South Africa prohibits discrimination on grounds of race; and so on. A big issue between New South Wales and Victoria when the Australian Constitution was drafted was where the new federal capital would be. The results can still be seen in section 125 of the Constitution, which provides that the capital shall be in New South Wales, but not within 100 miles of Sydney.

No constitution has everything to do with the running of government clearly written into it, however. Some rules which are very important to the workings of democratic government are found in other places as well: in Acts of Parliament, for example, or in decisions by courts. An example in Australia is the requirement for everyone to vote in elections, which is in an Act, but not in the Constitution. Also important are constitutional practices or "conventions" which are always (or almost always) followed, although they are not written into the Constitution or any law. The rule that the person who wins the election is appointed Prime Minister is one of these, at present. There are also many others, however, which will be described later in this book. The Constitution could not work without them.

2

Three important questions

A road-map

In a democracy, there are at least three things which people are likely to
want to know about the system of government. First, what kind of a say
do I have (along with everybody else)? Secondly, how are decisions
made? Thirdly, what are the limits on what governments may do and how
they may do it?

Asking these three questions is as good a way as any of getting to
understand the Australian constitutional system. This book is organised to
provide answers to them. This chapter provides an overview of them: a
road-map for what is to follow.

Having a say

Democracy is a system of government by the people, rather than by one
person or a few people who have complete power. It is not practical for all
decisions to be made by the people themselves, however. Even if it were
possible, it would be unlikely to happen, because most people have other
things to do, which interest them more. The challenge in designing a
democracy is to give people a real say, while allowing at least day-to-day
decisions to be made by others on their behalf. Chapters 6-15 of this book
describe how people have a say in Australia.

One obvious way of having a say is through voting in an election for
someone to represent you. In Australia, only the Parliaments and (usually)
local councils are elected. Even so, there are plenty of opportunities to
vote. Australia has different levels of government: Commonwealth, State
or Territory, and local government. Most Australians vote for
representatives at all three levels. In addition, the Commonwealth
Parliament has two "Houses" (the Senate and the House of
Representatives), both of which are elected. In all States except
Queensland the Parliament has two elected Houses as well.

Having a say through elections is important. It will not count for much, however, unless the elections are fair, your vote makes a difference and you know enough about what is going on to make a sensible choice. Australia does reasonably well on these points. It has a long tradition of fair elections. There is always a peaceful transfer of power when a government loses. Freedom of speech is valued and has some constitutional protection as well. Whether a single vote makes a difference is a more complicated question, as we will see when we look more closely at how we elect representatives, in Chapter 8.

There is another, quite different way in which people have a say in government. Australian voters much approve any change to the Australian Constitution. Some State Constitutions can be changed only by popular vote, or referendum as well. By and large, Australians expect to be consulted about constitutional change.

Making decisions

Many decisions are made for the community as a whole by elected representatives in governments and Parliaments. What these various bodies are, how they work and what they do are described in the second main part of the book, in Chapters 15 to 21.

In Australia, only Parliaments are directly elected, at the Commonwealth, State and Territory levels. Another name for a Parliament is a "legislature", or law-maker. Parliaments approve new laws and new taxes and agree to the spending of money raised from taxes. These are very significant decisions for running a government. It is appropriate for them to be made publicly and by all the elected representatives, acting together.

Parliament is too big to be the decision-maker on everything, however. Most decisions are made by a much smaller group which heads the executive government. This group consists of the Prime Minister (or Premier, in a State) and, say, 20 "Ministers", some or all of whom are members of "Cabinet". The Ministers in turn are assisted by the public service, which makes many decisions as well. Who these various people are and what they do are explained in Chapter 18.

The executive government cannot make law, but it suggests new laws to Parliament, which usually accepts them. It drafts a budget, with decisions about taxing and spending, which Parliament usually accepts also. In addition, the executive government acts in many other ways without referring to Parliament at all. Examples include appointing judges, making agreements or treaties with other countries, buying new ships for the navy or planes for the airforce, selling government businesses, or deciding that there should be or calling an election.

But this is a democracy, in which government is "by the people". If only the Parliament is elected, the executive government needs to be linked with it in some way. And it is. The executive government is formed from the party or group of parties (a "coalition") which has majority support in the House of Representatives – that is why Parliament usually accepts government proposals. All Ministers, or members of the executive government, are also Members of Parliament. If, for some reason, the government lost the support of the House of Representatives it would have to resign, or at least call an election. This is the system of government known as "responsible government". It is explained further in Chapter 16.

To understand how decisions are made in Australia, you need to take the different levels of government into account as well. The Constitution itself divides powers between the Commonwealth and the States. Chapter 20 describes how this is done. The States in turn give some of their power to local government. The Commonwealth makes decisions only on those matters given to it by the Constitution or which it can influence in some other way. Similarly, the States make decisions only on matters which the Constitution leaves to them. Sometimes, two or three levels of government take action in co-operation with each other. An increasing number of matters are dealt with in this way.

Some decisions also are made by courts, at both levels of government. Courts deal with disputes by applying the law. The law may be an Act passed by a Parliament, or a Constitution, which overrides all other laws. The law also includes the common law, made gradually by the judges themselves over the centuries, first in Britain and then in Australia, as they dealt with different cases. The way courts work is discussed in Chapter 19.

Limits

All democratic governments are limited in what they can do and how they can do it. This is not surprising. Representatives usually are required to act in a way that leaves some control with the people they represent and ensures that they are responsible to the people for their actions. Even in the case of a club, for example, this may involve some decisions being taken in public, others being reported to the members on a regular basis, approval of key decisions by the members themselves, and fairness in dealing with the rights or interests of individual members.

Government is different, of course. The "membership" is larger. Generally speaking, people do not "choose" to join. Governments have more control over their members or citizens, because they can enforce their actions through law. This needs to be taken into account in designing the limits on the way in which government itself acts.

Some of the main limits in Australia are described in Chapters 22 to 26. Briefly, they are these.

1.   We require government to act within the law, in much the same way as anybody else. This is known as the rule of law. To make it work properly and well, we need courts which are independent of government so that they will enforce the law equally and fairly, whoever the parties may be, even if one of the parties is the government.

2.   We also separate functions within government, so that no one part of government has too much power. This is sometimes referred to as separation of powers. Separation of powers means that only Parliaments make major new laws and only courts resolve legal disputes.

3.   Some constitutional systems, including ours, provide other "checks and balances" as well. The Senate is often a check on the House of Representatives. In very limited circumstances, the Head of State is a check on executive government. The federal system is another kind of check, because it limits what any one level of government can do.

All of these limits affect how governments act, not what they eventually do. But limits may be placed on what governments do as well. These generally are not necessary to protect a majority of the people. Where a democracy is working properly (and the Constitution can assist with this), governments can be expected to act in the interests of the majority.

Those whose interests may need greater protection, from governments or the majority itself, are individuals or minority groups. Is this undemocratic? Not necessarily. The very idea of democracy is based on ideas about the importance or value of each member of society. The value of each individual therefore should be respected in all decisions which a democratic government takes. There is room for disagreement about what this means in practice, but most of us would agree on a core of individual human rights.

There is another reason as well why a healthy, stable democracy requires respect for the rights and interests of others. Today's majority may be tomorrow's minority, and vice versa. Democracy relies on a peaceful transfer of power from one group to another, from time to time. That process would be less readily accepted, and might even be endangered, if people's most basic interests were at stake.

The rest of the book

Most of the rest of this book, beginning with Chapter 6, provides answers to these questions. First, however, it is necessary to introduce the Australian Constitution itself. How did we get it? In general, what is in it? And what has happened since it was first written to change the way in which it works? These introductory matters are covered in Chapters 3 to 5.

How did we get the Constitution?

An amazing achievement

The Australian Constitution was put together by agreement between Australians from all parts of the country. It took 10 years, from 1890 to 1 January 1901. It was an amazing achievement. To understand exactly what it meant, you need to know something about how Australia was governed before the Constitution was made.

Back to the beginning

Most of us tend to think of Australia's constitutional history as beginning in 1770, when Captain Cook discovered Australia or in 1788, when Governor Phillip established the first colony at Sydney Cove. This is because so much of our system of government can be traced to the British settlement of Australia – the location of our capital cities, the boundaries of the States, our legal system, the courts, Parliament, the monarchy.

Of course, Australian history goes back much earlier. Aboriginal people have been in Australia for at least 40,000 years. Over time, they developed their own rules to govern themselves, as all communities do.

Some of these rules, dealing with the relationship of Aboriginal groups to land, were recognised as part of Australian law in 1992 in the *Mabo* case by the High Court, which is Australia's highest court.

Separate or (partly) united?

The early British settlements in Australia were colonies, within the British Empire. There were two original colonies. New South Wales was settled in 1788. It covered the whole of the eastern part of the continent from north to south, including Tasmania. Western Australia was settled from 1829 and covered the whole western part, also from north to south.

The huge eastern colony of New South Wales gradually split apart as new communities were established or settlements which were a long way from Sydney argued that they should be allowed to govern themselves. Tasmania was first, in 1825. South Australia was founded in 1836. Victoria separated from New South Wales in 1851. Queensland was established in 1859. By this time, there were six separate colonies with systems of government of their own on the Australian mainland and in Tasmania.

Beyond their relationship with Britain (which is described in Chapter 5) these colonies had no formal links with each other. It was like having six separate countries in the area which we now know as Australia. This enabled the people of the colonies to make their own local decisions. But it created some problems as well. Each colony had its own defence force. They competed against each other for trade. They had separate road and railway systems. There were six postal services. Taxes were put on goods going from one colony to another. And yet the people of the colonies had a lot in common with each other. They also were a long way from the rest of the world. It seemed to make sense for them to try to get together, for particular purposes at least.

The main difficulty was a practical one. By 1890 each of the Australian colonies had its own Constitution, its own Parliament, its own government and its own courts. They were used to running their own affairs, with only occasional interference from Britain. No colony was likely to want to give this up entirely, even if that were desirable, in a country of this size. They needed a system of government which helped them to act jointly on some things and independently on others. And so they decided to form a federation.

What is a federation?

A federation enables separate communities to govern themselves in some matters while joining together to deal with other matters of mutual concern. People who live in a federation, therefore, will always be subject to two sets of government (and sometimes three, if there is local government as well). It is like a local sporting club, which belongs to a larger league. The local club and its members make some decisions for themselves. The league makes others, which affect the members in all the clubs which belong to it.

A federation was exactly what the Australian colonies thought they needed. They could form a national government (which became the Commonwealth) and give it responsibility for matters in which they wanted united action. But they could keep their own identity as well, as States (and eventually Territories). The Constitutions of the colonies, their systems of government and their laws would remain as the Constitutions, governments and laws of the States. A new national Constitution, the Australian Constitution, would override them all.

The Commonwealth and the six States are the main partners in the Australian federation. Since federation, Territories have been established as well. Some Territories have been given power to govern themselves. Two of them, the Northern Territory and the Australian Capital Territory, act like the States in most ways. They do not have the same independence as the States, however, because they are established by the Commonwealth and get their powers from it.

Who drew up the Australian Constitution?

Think about the problem of designing a Constitution in these circumstances.

It had to satisfy all the colonies, to persuade them all to join. Each colony had different needs and interests, however. And so each of them had different views about what the Constitution should say.

The Australian way of dealing with this was to give the task of drawing up the Constitution to a Convention.

A Convention was a meeting of representatives of the colonies. The advantages of a Convention were that it was small enough to work effectively, that it had a clear and defined purpose and that it had the authority to speak for the various colonies and their people.

The Constitution had to be acceptable to the British Government and Parliament as well, because only they could make the Constitution law. They had a chance to comment on the Constitution while it was being drafted and a final (small) say before it became law.

In the end, there were two Conventions. The National Australasian Convention met in Sydney, in 1891. It consisted of six delegates from each of the six Australian Parliaments and three from New Zealand, in case New Zealand was prepared to join the federation too. The Convention agreed on a Constitution. Its efforts came to nothing, however, because no further action was taken.

The second Convention was different. Most of the delegates were elected by popular vote (which was a lot less popular then than now, but was still impressive). The exceptions were Queensland which did not participate in this Convention and Western Australia which sent a delegation of Members of Parliament again. The New Zealanders were no longer involved.

The Australasian Federal Convention met in three separate sessions: in Adelaide and Sydney in 1897 and in Melbourne in 1898. The final draft on which they agreed was put to the voters for approval in all colonies (except Western Australia) before it was sent to Britain to be made law. The Western Australian voters agreed to it as well, before the Constitution came into effect, on 1 January 1901.

There are still signs of these events in the opening words of the Constitution: "Whereas the people of New South Wales, Victoria, South Australia, Queensland, and Tasmania ... have agreed to unite ...". Western Australia is missing, because the vote had not been taken there when the Commonwealth of Australian Constitution Act was passed by the British Parliament in 1900.

Writing the Constitution

The way used by the delegates to the Conventions for writing the Australian Constitution is a useful guide to writing a Constitution of any kind.

In the first place, they looked for other models, particularly for the federal part of the Constitution, which was new to them. There were several federations elsewhere in the world which they could use, but the main ones were the United States, Canada and Switzerland. They drew on all three, but in particular on the Constitution of the United States. Some of the delegates were familiar with the United States and this part of our Constitution is very closely based on theirs.

Secondly, the delegates to the Conventions agreed on some general principles or basic ideas, which set out what they wanted to achieve. These principles were a good indication of their priorities. For example, they wanted to be sure that trade between the colonies was "absolutely free" and that the new Commonwealth would take responsibility for defence for everyone. On the other hand, they did not want to give any more power to the Commonwealth than was necessary.

Once the principles were settled, the task of drafting the Constitution was left to committees, or smaller groups of Convention delegates. As soon as they had finished, the whole Convention met again to consider their work. The Convention went through the draft, section by section, making changes and voting on each one. Between the Adelaide and Sydney sessions they released the draft for comment by the colonial Parliaments and the British Government, and then met to discuss it again. Even after the final version was agreed, the Premiers of the colonies made a few more changes, which they thought were necessary to make sure that the Constitution was accepted.

The next chapter considers the content of the Constitution in greater detail.

4

What does the Constitution do?

Have a look at it

Have a look at the Constitution. It is easier to find your way around it if you understand how it is laid out.

The Constitution is divided into eight chapters. The first three are the easiest to remember. They deal respectively with the three main parts of government: the legislature or Parliament; the executive government, which includes the Queen and the Governor General and the Ministers; the courts or the "judicature". Within Chapter 1, on the Parliament, there are separate parts for the Senate and the House of Representatives.

Chapter 4 is called *Finance and Trade* and was once very important. It still has some key sections in it, including the guarantee of "absolute" freedom of trade between the States, to implement one of the main original principles agreed by the delegates to the Conventions. But a lot of Chapter 4 no longer operates. Sections 101-104, for example, refer to a body called the Interstate Commission, which does not now exist at all.

The title of Chapter 5 is *The States*. This chapter does not provide a complete constitutional framework for the States, however. For that, you need to look at the Constitutions of the States themselves. One of the main purposes of this chapter was to ensure that the Constitutions and laws of the colonies which had existed before federation continued to operate afterwards, when the colonies became "States". This chapter also contains the important section 109, which says that if there is conflict between Commonwealth and State laws, the Commonwealth law must be followed.

Chapter 6 is called *New States*. No new States have been created since the Constitution was written. Chapter 6 has been used a lot, however, because it gives the Commonwealth power to make laws for Australia's Territories. One of these, the Northern Territory would like to become a State, preferably in time for the centenary of the Constitution, in 2001, because a State has more independence. We are likely to hear more about Chapter 6 as those discussions proceed.

Chapter 7 is rightly described as *Miscellaneous*. It has only two sections now, since the section providing that "aboriginal natives shall not be counted" was removed in 1967. The first section in this chapter puts in place the historic compromise between New South Wales and Victoria about where the capital of Australia should be.

Chapter 8 has only one section, but it is a very important one: it describes how the Constitution itself can be changed and requires the approval of Australian voters for all changes.

At the front of your copy of the Constitution, before Chapter 1 begins, you will find the opening parts of the British Act which made the Constitution law. These first eight sections are called "covering clauses" to distinguish them from the first eight sections of the Constitution itself. Most of them no longer have any effect.

And right at the end of the Constitution you will find the promise or oath which all Members of the Commonwealth Parliament must make under section 42, before they begin work as Members of the House of Representatives or Senators.

Aims of the Constitution

If you draw up a Constitution, and in particular a Constitution for a country, you try to look ahead and anticipate the needs which will arise. You understand how important the Constitution is. And you also know that it is likely to last for a long time.

But, realistically, you give a lot of attention to immediate needs and immediate problems. If you do not deal with these, the Constitution may not be acceptable at all. Naturally also, in designing a Constitution, you draw on your own experiences. You think some things are too obvious to be written down. You include others, even if they are fairly minor, because you are worried about them. You know which issues are particularly sensitive and sometimes you avoid dealing with them at all.

And so it was with the Australian Constitution. The men who wrote or "framed" it knew they were writing a Constitution for a nation. They knew that the needs of the nation would change and they tried to anticipate these as best they could. But they were men of their own times and they had to respond to immediate needs.

So, for example, the framers did not think that it was necessary to describe how the powers of the Governor-General would be exercised, or to mention the Prime Minister or Cabinet, because they assumed that everyone would understand how this part of the Constitution was supposed to work. They made detailed arrangements for matters which particularly concerned them (for example, railways) which we would think less important today. They could not agree on how to divide money between the Commonwealth and the States and so they left the problem unresolved.

Their aims for the Constitution were driven by the needs of the moment as well. To be of any use at all, the Constitution had to do at least two things. It had to bring the colonies – preferably all six of them – together in a federal system and to make it as clear as possible what each government could do. And it had to create a new system of government, for the new Commonwealth of Australia. Both of these aims were difficult enough and so took most of their attention.

What about us?

The Australian Constitution says very little about people.

In one sense this is odd. In a democracy, the authority of government is supposed to come from the people. Most Australians believe that people have basic rights to liberty, to equality before the law and to freedom of speech, opinion and belief, amongst others. These principles are written into the Constitutions of many other countries throughout the world. So why are they not in ours?

For different reasons. Our system of government has always left a lot to be decided by executive governments and parliaments from time to time. Historically, as our constitutional tradition developed, it emphasised the role of Parliament, rather than of the people whom Parliament represents. Australians value individual rights and liberties, but tend to assume that they will be respected whether we give them constitutional protection or not.

The framers of the Constitution made these assumptions, much as we do today. But standards were different when the Constitution was drafted anyway. There was less concern then about the need to protect minorities from majorities. Racial discrimination was more acceptable. The Constitution required discrimination against the Aboriginal people, in a section which was not removed until 1967. And while Australia was ahead of much of the rest of the world in giving the vote to women, agreement on this issue was not reached in time to include it in the Constitution. There are still signs of that unfinished debate in the third paragraph of section 128.

This is not to suggest that the Constitution has nothing to say about people. With only a little bit of imagination the opening words of the Constitution Act (the preamble) can be interpreted to mean that the Constitution draws its authority from the people. The High Court has said that there are some limits on government power to interfere with the freedom of Australians to speak about political matters. A few other sections expressly limit government power in ways which effectively protect individuals. Australians are entitled to compensation if their property is acquired under Commonwealth law. The Commonwealth cannot interfere with religious beliefs. No State can treat a resident of another State worse than it treats its own.

These arrangements or provisions are the exceptions rather than the rule, however. Generally, the Australian Constitution deals with structures of government rather than with relations between governments and the people. This may be one reason why Australians are said to be less interested in it.

The age of the Constitution

One of the main functions of a Constitution is to state and protect the rules about government which are considered to be most important by the people who will be governed by them.

Constitutions are designed to last. But as times change, views about what is important and what is not may change as well. Eventually this change may be so great as to affect the usefulness of the Constitution.

The Australian Constitution is almost one hundred years old. This makes it one of the oldest written Constitutions in the world. The next chapter asks the question: what has happened in the past 100 years which might affect our view of what should be in the Constitution and what it should say?

5

Changing times

The range of change

Of course, a lot has happened since the Constitution came into effect in
1901, both within Australia and outside it. For example, cars were not in
general use until after federation. The first aeroplane flew in Australia in
1909. Radio and television are inventions of the 20th century.

Changes of this kind have affected our lives. They also make us appreciate
the age of the Constitution, because we are so used to this technology and
it is not mentioned directly in the Constitution. In fact, however, the
Constitution has adapted reasonably well to all of these changes as,
indeed, you would expect it to do. Air travel is covered largely by the
Commonwealth's responsibility for overseas and interstate trade. The
States deal with cars and roads, but they co-operate over national roads
and interstate transport. As it happens, radio and television come under an
unusual section of the Constitution, which gives the Commonwealth
Parliament power to pass laws for "Postal, telegraphic, telephonic *and
other like services*". Many years ago, the High Court said that radio and
television were "like" enough to posts and telegraphs to fall within this
power.

Not all changes are so easily taken care of, however. Changes in what
people believe is important may affect the Constitution, if they alter what
Australians want the Constitution to do. Changes in the assumptions
which were made when the Constitution was written, or to the context in
which it works, may have an impact as well.

To understand how different types of change may affect a Constitution in
different ways, think about the constitution for a football club. It probably
would not be affected by minor changes to the rules of the game, or to the
number of teams, or to the number of clubs in the League. But if the club
moved to a different league, or merged with another club, or wanted to set

itself up as a company or planned to run a health farm as well it would be necessary to look at the constitution again.

Some changes which have taken place since federation, which may be relevant to the Australian Constitution, are considered elsewhere in this book. The rest of this chapter deals with one particular change: Australia's transition from colony to independent nation.

Australia becomes independent

Australia was a group of six colonies within the British Empire when the Constitution was drafted. The Commonwealth of Australia also was a colony when the Constitution came into effect. Even then, Australians made decisions for themselves on most matters, as the story of the drafting of the Constitution shows. What being a colony meant, however, was that final authority over decisions of Australian governments or Parliaments or courts lay in Britain. Acts of the British Parliament could overrule Australian Acts. Decisions of the British Privy Council (a final appeal court for the colonies) could make decisions of Australian courts no longer valid. The King or Queen was represented in Australia by a Governor-General and by State Governors, and the British government could influence the action which they took on particular matters. And relations with other countries were handled by Britain on behalf of all of its colonies, including Australia.

This situation began to change almost immediately after federation. The process was so gradual, however, that it is impossible to identify a particular date as the moment of Australia's independence.

One key date was 1926, when it was formally recognised by both the British and Australian governments that, in real, day-to-day terms, Australia was no longer a colony, so that the Governor-General should no longer act on British advice (and nor should the King or Queen, in Australian affairs).

Another important date was 1942, when the Commonwealth Parliament passed the Statute of Westminster Adoption Act to recognise its own independence from the British Parliament and British laws. The process of independence was completed for the Commonwealth when appeals to the

Privy Council from federal courts were ended in two stages, in 1968 and 1975.

Yet another key date was 1986 when the Australia Acts were passed, breaking all further legal links between Australia and Britain and making it clear that the British Parliament could no longer make laws or legislate for any part of Australia.

By 1986 at the latest, therefore (and in practice, much earlier) Australia was a fully independent nation, with its own interests and priorities, governing itself and playing a full international role as well.

What about the Constitution?

Australian independence was achieved through constitutional conventions or practices and legislation of the British, Australian and State Parliaments. There was no change to the Australian Constitution at all.

This was possible because the Constitution (or the relevant parts of it) was so general that it could be adapted readily to the new situation.

For example, the Constitution did not specify who would advise the Queen or King and the Governor-General, or even require them to act on advice at all. It was easy enough in these circumstances for governments simply to agree that in future the advice would come only from Australians.

Appeals to the Privy Council were ended under the Constitution itself. Section 74 allowed the Commonwealth Parliament to "limit" appeals from the High Court to the Privy Council. In 1975, the Parliament used the power to end appeals entirely, and the High Court agreed that it could do so.

Lingering signs

Despite the Constitution's ability to adapt to these new circumstances, it still shows signs of Australia's original colonial identity.

One of the most obvious is the legal form of the Constitution. As we noted in Chapter 2, the Australian Constitution is section 9 of a British statute, the Commonwealth of Australia Constitution Act 1900. In 1900 the

Australians thought that it was necessary for the British Parliament to make the Constitution into law, because Britain still had final authority over Australia. Nowadays, we prefer to remember that the Australian people approved the draft first and we tend to forget the British Act. But the opening words or preamble and the eight covering clauses of our Constitution are a continuing reminder of it.

Another reminder of the past which is the subject of present debate is the position of the Queen as Australian Head of State. The argument here is more complex. It is unlikely that Australia would have made a King or Queen its Head of State if it had been independent at the time. On the other hand, the Queen is now officially the "Queen of Australia." For many Australians, this makes the monarchy an Australian institution which is relevant to present-day Australia.

Some of the constitutional powers of the Queen are undoubtedly colonial in character, however, and would not have been included in a Constitution for an independent Australia.

The most well known of these is section 59 which gives the Queen power to overrule or "disallow" any Commonwealth law within one year after it has been made. The power has never been used, and certainly would not be used now.

Another example is section 2, which gives the Governor-General "such powers and functions of the Queen as Her Majesty may be pleased to assign to him". Powers have been given to the Governor-General under the section (some quite recently), but it is unlikely that this section will be used any longer. We now assume that the Commonwealth has all the executive power that it needs under the Constitution itself.

An example of a different kind is the guarantee in section 117 of equal treatment for all interstate residents who are "subjects of the Queen". This is no longer read literally so as to give, for example, Canadians and New Zealanders better treatment than Italians or Chinese. If we had to justify this we would probably argue that "Queen" now means the "Queen of Australia". Nevertheless, the reference now looks odd.

Omissions

It is interesting to think about additional provisions which we might have put into a Constitution for an independent Australia.

We might, for example, have said something about Australia's independence in the preamble. Or, if we took independence for granted, we might have said something about Australia's identity, and the role we seek to play in the world. As the Constitution would not have needed to be supported by the British Act, the preamble would have come at the start of the Constitution itself. It might also have said directly that the Constitution draws its authority from the people.

We might also have included something about citizenship in the Constitution: who is an Australian citizen, and the rights which citizens have. As we will see in Chapter 6, the framers of the Constitution considered whether to include a reference to Australian citizenship, but in the end they decided against it. They had a mixture of motives for this. At least one, however, was uncertainty about what Australian citizenship meant, when Australia was still a colony.

If Australia had been independent when the Constitution was written, we probably also would have said more about how agreements or treaties are made with other countries, and how they take effect within Australia. There was a mention of treaties in an early draft of the Constitution, but it was taken out, because Australia was not then allowed to conduct its own international relations.

As Australia became independent, we simply assumed that the general "executive power" in section 61 includes the power to make treaties as well. After a while, the power of the Commonwealth Parliament to legislate for "external affairs", which was considered quite unimportant in 1901, expanded also, to allow the Parliament to put into effect any treaty which Australia has agreed to.

This last development was controversial. The expansion of the external affairs power enabled the Commonwealth or overrule more State laws. In recent years, we have also begun to question whether executive governments should be able to make international commitments on behalf of Australia without any involvement of the Parliament (or the people) at all.

So far, we have dealt with these difficulties informally, by promising discussion on treaties between the Commonwealth and the States and by allowing the Parliament to comment on treaty proposals. If we were writing the Constitution today, however, we probably would try to meet these concerns in the text of the Constitution itself.

6

We the people

Popular sovereignty

It is sometimes said that in Australia (or in any democracy) the "people" are sovereign. Sovereignty means final authority or power. Popular sovereignty means that final authority in a constitutional system lies with the people themselves.

But what does this really mean? It might mean no more than that the people can change the government at an election, by voting for different Members of Parliament. This would give the people "political sovereignty" (as long as the elections were fair). Once elected, however, the Parliament would have the final authority, because only the Parliament can make or change laws.

In fact, in Australia, popular sovereignty means more than this. As we saw in Chapter 3, the Australian Constitution originally was approved by the people themselves. In these circumstances, it is possible to argue that the Constitution and the whole system of government which it sets up rests on the authority of the people. There is a reminder of this in the opening words of the preamble. The argument gets further support from the fact that the Constitution cannot now be changed without the approval of the people.

Nor does Parliament have final legal authority in Australia. All Parliaments, both Commonwealth and State, must act within the limits of the Constitution, as interpreted by the High Court. Parts of the Constitution protect the democratic process and further reinforce the authority of the voters.

There are other ways of giving greater effect to the authority of the people in a democracy. One which is sometimes discussed is "direct" democracy, in which the people make some decisions themselves by voting on particular issues. Direct democracy tends to be controversial, because of a fear that the power might be abused. There are obvious difficulties also in helping voters to understand issues which are technical or complex. Until now, we have been able to dismiss direct democracy as a way of making decisions because it is impractical and expensive as well. Information technology will soon make it possible for us to vote from home, however. Eventually we will need to decide whether we want more direct democracy and, if so, in what circumstances it can properly be used.

Who are the people?

At any one time, the Australian community is made up of a wide range of different people, with different rights and different responsibilities in the constitutional system. Some are tourists or other short-term visitors. Some are very old, or very young. Some live here permanently and some are only here for a period of time. Some are Australian citizens, but many are not.

Which of these do we mean when we talk about "the people"? That depends on the context.

Everyone in Australia is entitled to basic rights: protection of the law, for example.

Members of Parliament have a responsibility to everyone in the area they represent (their electorate) and not just to the people who vote for them. People who migrated to Australia and have made it their home are entitled to the services which the government provides to the rest of the community, even if they have not become citizens and cannot vote. Young Australians deserve special care, because they do not yet have the full capacity to look after themselves.

But the central group of "the people" are those who have the right to participate actively in Australian democracy, by voting in elections and in referendums, and by taking part in political life by standing for election themselves. Without these people, there would be no democracy at all. The question of who has these rights therefore is extremely important.

Citizens

In the 1990s it is possible to say that, in general, all Australian citizens have full political rights, once they have become adults. They can temporarily lose them for some reason (for example, if they are in prison for a serious crime). Otherwise, however, we generally accept that all citizens are full members of the Australian political community and that all people who can vote and stand for election are Australian citizens.

How does someone become a citizen? Most people become citizens of their country automatically, because of the circumstances in which they were born. Different countries have slightly different rules, however. In Australia, if your parents are citizens, you are likely to be a citizen too. Other people become citizens of a country by choice, at a later stage in life, by meeting whatever conditions that country lays down. So, in Australia, it is possible to become a citizen if you have lived here for two of the past five years (and met some other statutory requirements).

This neat link between citizenship and basic political rights has not always been there, however. Women did not vote throughout Australia until 1908, although they were "Australians" in every other sense. Aboriginal Australians did not vote in federal elections until 1962. Some British people, who are not Australian citizens, are able to vote in Australia because they had the vote here many years ago and we thought it unfair to take it away. On the other hand, as we will see in Chapter 13, some Australian citizens are not allowed to stand for election, because they are citizens of another country as well.

And the link between citizens and voting may not always be so clear in the future. People are moving between countries a lot more than they used to, for many different reasons. If this continues (as seems likely) we may eventually decide to allow people who are here permanently or for a long period of time to vote in some elections, in the interests of the health of our own democratic community.

What does the Constitution say?

If the question "who has these rights" is so important, should the Constitution provide an answer, or guidelines of some kind?

If we were writing the Constitution today, it probably would. Even 100 years ago, the framers of the Constitution discussed whether to mention Australian citizenship in it. Many of them wanted to do so, because they thought that the Constitution should state what it meant to be a member of this large new nation, which they were creating.

But in the end, they decided not to. Remember that Australia was a colony at the time. Like people in other parts of the British Empire, Australians were "subjects" of the Crown (the word used for people who are ruled by a monarch). There was no separate legal identity or status of Australian citizen, and the framers hesitated to create one. And they were not sure that they wanted to create one anyway. There was some danger that "citizens" would be regarded as equals. This would have interfered with some of the laws then in force, which discriminated on the grounds of race.

The Constitution therefore does not mention Australian citizenship. Nor, as we will see in Chapter 13, does it give anyone the right to vote or to stand for Parliament. The idea of Australian citizenship developed when Australia became independent. The rules about how you become a citizen are described in an Act of Parliament, and could be changed by another Act of Parliament.

The reasons why the framers decided not to mention citizenship in the Constitution no longer exist. There is no reason why citizenship should not be mentioned now, to identify the "core" of the people on whom Australian democracy relies and to ensure that the rights of Australian citizens, at least, are constitutionally secure. Before we did that, however, we would need to agree on the rights which should be attached to citizenship. This issue is discussed again later, in Chapter 13.

The future

The question of who are "the people" who have full political rights is linked to our idea of democracy. Both have changed over time, generally in the direction of including more people in our political community. Even in the past 100 years, since the Australian Constitution was written, the community has expanded to include Australian women, then Aboriginal Australians, then young Australians aged between 18 and 21.

So far, however, "the people" are limited to Australian citizens, for the purposes of voting and standing for election. This is appropriate in a world made up of countries whose populations are fairly stable. The more mobile people become, however, the less appropriate it may seem to be.

In due course we may need to think about the following questions. Should Australian citizens be able to vote in Australian elections, even though they live (permanently) elsewhere? Should people who are not Australian citizens, but who have lived here for a long time be able to vote, or even to stand for election? Should we recognise, more broadly than we already do, that people may, quite properly, be citizens of more than one country? And in that case, will we allow them to use political rights in both countries, or either country, as they choose?

The idea of Parliament

What is a Parliament?

However democratic our system of government may be, we cannot all govern, or at least not on a day-to-day basis. There are too many of us to make decisions quickly. Many government decisions are complex and need to be made by someone who has the time and interest to identify all the issues and decide how they should be settled. And it is important that the interests of the whole community are thought about when government decisions are made. This may be less likely to happen, if the people take the decisions themselves.

For all these reasons, we elect representatives to make most government decisions for us. The representatives we elect form a Parliament and we call them Members of Parliament. Because Parliament is the only directly elected body, we require it to make or approve all the most important decisions. This is the reason why only Parliament can change the law, require you to pay taxation and agree to the spending of the money collected from these taxes.

Even Parliament is too big to make many of the necessary decisions, however. We also need an "executive" government, to run things on a regular basis and to plan ahead. Different countries choose their executive government in different ways. In the United States, for example, the executive is directly elected, separately from the law-making body (which they call "Congress"). By contrast, in Australia, the main part of the executive comes from the Parliament. Whoever has the support (or the "confidence") of the Parliament becomes the Prime Minister and the Ministers. The ministry is responsible to the Parliament for what they do and how they do it. In this way, even though we do not directly elect executive government, they are our representatives too.

Where did the idea of Parliament come from?

The Australian Parliaments are modelled on the British Parliament, which can be traced back to a time well before democratic government began.

The first Parliaments met in the 13th or 14th centuries, more than 600 years ago. That was a time when monarchs had the real power to govern. Parliaments were called together by the ruling King or Queen to consider and (hopefully) to approve new taxes or other proposals which the monarch wanted to introduce. The monarch did not necessarily need Parliament's approval. Even in those days, however, it was helpful to get the support of the representatives of some of the people who would be affected by the changes to be made.

Gradually, the relationship between the monarch and Parliament shifted. Eventually, it came to be accepted that new taxes and new laws always required the approval of Parliament; that Parliament must meet regularly (at least every year); and that all the powers of the monarch had to be exercised on the advice of a Prime Minister and Ministers whom the Parliament was prepared to support. As Parliaments gained power, monarchs gradually lost it. For most of the 20th century, the monarch has had almost no real power at all.

The Members of these early Parliaments were regarded as representatives. They represented only a small proportion of the people, however, and the methods by which they were chosen would not now be regarded as satisfactory. The ideas that all adult citizens (at least) are entitled to vote and that elections should be regular and fair were not fully accepted until the 20th century.

Outwardly, Parliament did not change much at all over this long period. But in fact it was very different. It now represented a much larger range of people, with widely different interests and needs. And it was the only institution through which the idea that government draws its authority from the people could be put into practice.

This history explains why, even now, there are such apparently close links between Parliament and the Queen (or, in Australia, the Governor-General and State Governors). If you look at section 1 of the Constitution, for example, you will see that the Queen is part of the Commonwealth

22

2222222222222222222

Parliament. Under section 58 her "assent" or agreement is given to laws passed by the House of Representatives and the Senate. Under sections 5 and 28 the Governor-General calls Parliament together, brings sessions to an end (or "prorogues" Parliament) and dissolves (or breaks up) the House of Representatives, to bring on new elections.

These are leftovers of powers which, historically, the monarch exercised over Parliament. Today, they are not real powers at all, because (almost) all of them are carried out or exercised on the advice of the government. An important current question is whether the Head of State should still have these powers or whether some of them could be exercised in another way, or abolished altogether. Do we still need someone to "assent" to legislation, for example, if assent is automatically given?

What does being a representative mean?

We say that Members of Parliament "represent" the people in their electorates and that Parliament "represents" the people as a whole. In practice, though, what do we expect this to mean?

The same question arises (although the answer may be different) whenever one person is chosen to represent others: on a student council, for example, or a union executive. One possibility is that we vote for people because we trust them more than the other candidates or because we like what they seem to believe in or stand for. Once elected, however, we accept that they must do whatever they think is best. Another, quite different, possibility is that we expect our representatives to do what we want them to do or what we would do if we were in their place.

Representation in Parliament is closer to the first of these, although it has some elements of both. Generally, we accept that Members of Parliament can act as they think best, once elected. We cannot tell in advance what issues will come up, so they need this freedom of action. In any case, they are supposed to act in everyone's interests, not just in yours or mine or in the interests of the people who voted for them. If enough of us dislike what is done, we can vote someone else in as a representative at the next election.

Representatives cannot do just as they please, however. Many of us vote one way or another because of what candidates said they would do if they were elected. If they break these promises, without good reason, voters understandably are annoyed. In any event, Members of Parliament are likely to be influenced by public opinion, because they want to be re-elected. If you have a problem with a government decision, or a point of view of your own to express, you have the right to expect your Member of Parliament to listen to you and to help if he or she reasonably can.

Representation in Parliament is made more complicated by the role which political parties play. A political party is an organised group which puts forward candidates for election and develops policies to be followed if enough of its candidates are elected to form a government. Almost every Member of Parliament is elected as a candidate for one of a small number of parties (Liberal Party, Australian Labor Party, Australian Democrats, National Party).

Parties help to make parliamentary government work. They present voters with clear alternative policies. They ensure that there will (almost always) be a majority to support the government's proposals. But they also affect the relationship between voters and their representatives in Parliament. Members of Parliament are bound to do what their party has decided to do. Most people now vote for candidates because they prefer the particular party to which that person belongs. They expect the party to stick by its election promises, but otherwise to do whatever it thinks best.

The authority of Parliament

The idea of Parliament assumes that a majority of voters elect the Members of Parliament and that decisions of the Parliament are made by a majority of Members. This does not necessarily mean that decisions of Parliament actually represent "the will of the people", but it gives decisions of Parliament great authority, all the same. In some systems of government it is accepted to give Parliament absolute authority, or "parliamentary sovereignty". In these systems, whatever Parliament decides becomes law and is required to be given effect.

There are various reasons why Parliament may not be given final authority, however. A society may want to protect the basic or funda-mental features of the system of government from changes by Parliament alone. This could include the rules by which Members of Parliament are chosen. A society may choose to protect certain concerns of minority groups or of individuals from decisions of a majority in Parliament. If the people, rather than the Parliament, is accepted as "sovereign" it may be appropriate for some things to be done only by the people, rather than by their representatives in Parliament. Usually, restrictions of this kind are included in a Constitution and limit what Parliament can do.

Usually also, it is a court (in Australia, the High Court) which decides whether Parliament has gone beyond its limits. There is a possibility for conflict between a court which is enforcing the Constitution and a Parliament which says it represents the current majority of the people. A very delicate balance needs to be kept between the two, in which each respects the role of the other.

What room is there for us?

The idea of Parliament tends to assume that voters have a say at election time, but that in between elections, decisions are left to their representatives alone.

In practice, of course, the situation is more complex. Voters are entitled to expect their representatives to keep the promises which they made during the election campaign, believing that the promises were made responsibly in the first place. Members of Parliament pay attention to public opinion, because they want to win the next election. Members who won at the last election by only a small number of votes are likely to pay particular attention to what voters in their areas think.

But is this all there is to it? Should people have more of a say between elections? There is no clear answer to this in principle. It depends on what we choose our representatives to do.

But there may be practical reasons why people should play a greater role. Laws should meet real needs, if they are to be effective. People will obey laws more readily if they understand them and think that they are workable and fair. Representatives need to draw on the knowledge and views of the people they represent between elections, in order to do their job properly. People are more likely to support the system of government (although not necessarily a particular government) if they have the opportunity to take part in the decisions which are made.

The difficulty is to put this ideal of participation into practice without making it too hard for governments to make good decisions quickly, in the interests of us all. At present, we expect governments and Parliaments to consult with the main organisations representing different groups of people, when making decisions which affect their members: for example, business, unions, aged persons' groups, farmers, indigenous representatives, and so on. Increasingly, other forms of public participation are beginning to be used as well. Some parliamentary committees (groups within parliament who deal with particular issues, such as health or education) advertise for public comments on proposed new laws, or Bills, before they are made. More recently, public comments sometimes have been asked for on international treaties, before Australia agrees to them. The internet could provide more opportunities for public participation in government decision-making. Already, a great deal of information about government is available on the internet. It is likely to become a way in which government gets information and ideas from the community as well, over time.

Electing representatives

The importance of elections

Obviously, elections are very important in a parliamentary system, even if we can participate in government in other ways as well. Elections decide which people, belonging to which parties, will represent us in Parliament. In Australia they decide who will form the government. They provide one particular time for the voters to have their say.

There are different kinds of election systems to choose from, and each has different effects. Some systems make it more likely that a single party will win a majority of seats in Parliament. Some systems make sure that a wider range of views will be reflected in Parliament, but make it more difficult to form a government and to keep it together. Some systems elect one Member for a particular area. Others choose a number of Members for a larger area. Some systems save special seats for minority groups which might not otherwise be represented at all. Some systems have elections every two or three years. Some have elections every four or five years.

How do we know which of these options to choose? Most countries, including Australia, try to find a system which will allow both effective government and fair representation. The rest of this chapter describes the options in a bit more detail and the choices which Australia has made.

Voting system

A central issue for any election system is the way in which votes are counted.

Consider, for example, a community in which there are one million voters, and four political parties. Party A usually gets 40% of the vote, party B gets 30%, party C gets 20% and party D gets 10%. Assume also (to make the example easier) that there are only 10 places or "seats" in the Parliament for this community.

The fairest outcome of an election in these circumstances would be one which gave party A four seats, party B three seats, party C two seats and party D one seat. There are election systems which will do this. This method of counting votes is known as "proportional representation". If this method were used, however, no one party would have a majority of seats in the Parliament, so as to be able to make decisions easily. To form a majority government, one party would need to co-operate with another, or even with two. This is called a "coalition".

There are other systems which would make it more likely that elections in this community would give one party a majority of seats, so as to form a majority government.

Assume, in our example, that the community is divided into 10 areas for the purpose of elections, each area electing one Member. Also assume that they use a voting method in which the person who gets the most votes in his or her area wins the seat. If support for each of the parties were even across all groups (which in practice would be unlikely), party A would win all ten seats, with 40% of the vote in each. This would be a very unsatisfactory result, from the standpoint of parliamentary government. There would be no representation of the people who voted for parties B, C and D. The government would be supported by only 40% of the voters. The election results would be clear, however, and the government certainly would be very stable. This system of voting is known as "First Past the Post".

Australia has developed a variation of this, which is used in the House of Representatives and in some State Houses of Parliament. When we vote in an election for one of these Houses, we are asked to list who we would like to win, or our preferences, starting with our first choice and then marking who our second choice is and so on. If one person standing for election ("candidate") gets 50% of the vote or more, they will win the election. If not, preferences are considered before the winner of the seat is decided. This can have a huge effect on the outcome. In the case of our imaginary community, for example, if the supporters of parties C and D preferred party B to party A, party B would win. This system still tends to produce a clear majority in the Parliament, but also gives more weight to the preferences of voters. It is sometimes called preferential voting.

Electoral divisions

In designing any election system, there is a further question about whether the whole community should choose all the Members to be elected or whether the community should be divided up in some way.

Take Australia as an example. Assume that we want to elect 148 Members to the House of Representatives (which is roughly the actual size of the House). Should we all vote for the whole 148? Or should we work out the number of Members to be elected from each State or Territory (say, 37 from Victoria) and require all the voters in each State (or Territory) to vote for all the Members from that State? Or should we divide Australia into smaller areas still, so that a smaller number of voters elect a smaller number of Members, or perhaps only one Member? When this is done, the smaller areas are called electorates, or electoral divisions.

In Australia, we use electoral divisions, each electing one Member, for the House of Representatives and for some State Houses of Parliament. In other words, we divide the country, or the State, into as many electorates as there are Members. The number of Members, in turn, is decided by the relevant Constitution, in one way or another. This system has its advantages. It would be hard for us to vote for 148 people nationwide, or even 37 people statewide, because we would not have any idea who they are. The use of divisions ensures that Members come from all parts of the country and not just from the largest States or from capital cities. It means that each Member is directly responsible to more or less the same number of voters and that voters know who "their" Member is (or, at least, can find out easily enough).

There are disadvantages of the system as well, however. In the first place, proportional representation does not work in single-Member electoral divisions. For this reason Tasmania and the Australian Capital Territory have created larger divisions, called multi-member electorates, each electing 5-7 Members. Multi-Member electorates also make it more likely that every voter will have at least one Member from the party for which he or she voted. Voters may be more comfortable about taking problems to their Member in these circumstances.

Pre-selection

Who stands for election to Parliament? Where do the candidates come from?

Anyone can stand for Parliament if they meet the legal requirements and pay the necessary money or deposit. But, these days, most Members of Parliament are also members of a political party. In that case, it is the party which decides who will stand for election, according to its rules. This is called "pre-selection". The party then supports its candidates through the election process to try to make sure that they win.

In some cases, pre-selection for a particular party means that you are almost certain to win the seat. Some electorates are "safe" for one party or another, because a large majority of the voters in the electorate always support that party. Other electorates are "marginal". The seat sometimes is won by one party and sometimes by another. A very small number of voters may decide the outcome, in these cases. All parties devote a lot of attention to marginal seats, because they are easier to win, or to lose.

Pre-selection raises some difficult issues for representative democracy. On the one hand, there is an important principle that people should be able to form political parties and that parties should be able to make their own decisions. On the other hand, the candidates chosen by the parties are the people for whom, eventually, the rest of us will vote. If the parties choose badly, or unfairly, or unwisely, that will affect the quality of our democracy and system of government. Should the pre-selection process be made more public or accountable in some way? Or can we leave these decisions to the parties alone, on the assumption that it is in their own interests to select the best candidates they can?

Representing different groups

Our system of representative government tends to assume that anyone can represent anyone else. If you are elected to Parliament under the name of a particular party, you must take decisions in accordance with the rules of that party, which in turn should take into account the interests of the whole community.

Nevertheless, we worry when Parliament does not appear representative. In recent years there has been concern that there are not enough women in Parliament. There are only a small number of Members of Parliament from groups which have come to Australia since the second world war. And there have been hardly any indigenous Australians in the national Parliament at all.

Does this matter? The answer is yes, if the quality of representation is not as good as it could or should be. If Members of Parliament have a wider range of experiences, their decisions should be better informed. If Members of Parliament come only from particular parts of the community, Parliament might seem less relevant to other parts. A broadly representative Parliament could provide a model of how different people can work together in the common interest for the sake of everyone. It could also encourage a wider range of people to stand for election to Parliament themselves.

It is more difficult to work out how to make Parliament more representative. One answer, again, is to leave it to the political parties, hoping that their interest in winning elections will encourage them to broaden their range of candidates. There is also the choice of a different voting method, based on proportional representation, which would make it easier to make sure that a wider range of people are elected. Another option is to provide some seats in Parliament specifically for groups who do not receive enough or any representation through the normal election methods. New Zealand, for example, presently sets aside five seats in its House of Representatives for Maori New Zealanders.

Timing of elections

One final question about elections is how often they should be held. If the time or interval between elections is too long, representatives may lose the support of the voters and will not be properly accountable to them. The longer the period between elections, the more important it is for people to have the chance to influence government decisions and for the processes of government to be as open as possible. On the other hand, if the interval between elections is too short, representatives will spend too much time worrying about the next election, instead of getting on with governing.

Most Parliaments in the world today have elections at intervals of between 3 to 5 years. Australia is towards the shorter end of this, with elections every three years for the House of Representatives and every three or four years for State Parliaments. One current issue is whether the term (length of time between elections) of the House of Representatives should be longer. The arguments for and against are the familiar ones: fair representation on the one hand and effective government on the other. As we will see below in Chapter 11 there is also a complication about the terms of Senators, if the term of the House of Representatives is increased.

One argument should be dismissed at once, however. It is sometimes said that the interval between elections should be longer because Australians are sick of voting. If this is true, it is a serious situation and we should try to work out what the real problem is. Even if elections were held every year they would not be particularly time-consuming and would be a small price to pay for government through people who truly represent us.

9

The Australian Parliaments

There are nine Parliaments in Australia

Every Australian elects representatives to two Parliaments. One is the Australian, or Commonwealth, Parliament. It makes laws for all Australians, in areas of Commonwealth responsibility. It gives the authority for the executive government of the Commonwealth. It is set up and described by the Australian Constitution, and meets in Canberra.

Each of us also elects representatives to the Parliament of the State or Territory in which we live. These are set up by the relevant State Constitution or, in the case of the Territories, by their Self-Government legislation. They meet in the capital city of the State or the Territory. They make laws in matters which the Constitution leaves to the States or which the Commonwealth has given to the Territories. They give the authority for the State or Territory government.

The main reason why Australia has two sets of Parliaments in this way is that we have a federal system. Federalism divides power between two levels, or spheres, of government. Each government, at each level, has a Parliament.

The number of governments and Parliaments in Australia is sometimes criticised, because we have a small population.

Multiple Parliaments have some advantages in terms of democracy, however. They give Australians more of a chance to have a say in the business of government, through elections. They mean that everyone has at least two "local Members", one Commonwealth and one State, who may even be from different parties. State and Territory Parliaments also make sure there are elected representatives closer than Canberra to the people who elected them. In large States like Queensland and Western Australia, however, even the State Parliaments can still be far away .

The model for Australian Parliaments

All Australian Parliaments roughly follow the example or model of the British Parliament. This is the result of our history. As the colonies began to govern themselves, it was natural for them to set up Parliaments like those they already understood.

Because they followed the same model, all Australian Parliaments operate in more or less the same way.

Their Members generally fall into two groups, Government (the party with the majority) and Opposition. Occasionally there are a few Members who belong to smaller parties or who come from no party as well.

All Parliaments accept that their function is to make new laws, to make decisions about taxing and spending and to make the government accountable through, for example, asking questions in Parliament.

The rights or "privileges" of all Members of Parliament are broadly the same. We accept, for example, that Members should be able to say whatever they like in Parliament, although we hope that they use this privilege responsibly.

And the methods for making new laws are much the same as well. A suggested or proposed law is always introduced into a Parliament in the form of a "Bill". It goes through at least three stages or "readings" in each House. The Governor-General must give each Bill the "royal assent" before it becomes an "Act". The most important of these stages is the "Second Reading" where the Minister responsible for the Bill describes its purpose and the Opposition Member, who "shadows" this Minister by taking an interest in the same matters, says what the Opposition thinks about the proposal. Other Members then make comments as well. You can read what Members of Parliament have said about any Bill in the published record of parliamentary debates. This sometimes is called Hansard, after the printers in Britain who began to publish parliamentary debates there in the early 19th century.

Members of each House vote on whether to accept a Bill or not at both the second and third reading stages. They usually vote in the way their party wishes, which means that a Bill which the government has introduced will almost always pass because the government represents the party with the most votes. Very occasionally, parties allow their Members a "free" or "conscience" vote on a Bill. Members may vote in accordance with their own beliefs or, perhaps, the preferences of their electorate, and the party has no fixed view. This happened, for example, in 1997 when the Commonwealth Parliament voted on whether to overturn the Northern Territory legislation making it legal to help people who were terminally ill to die.

All lower Houses of Parliament are managed or chaired by a "Speaker", whose job it is to ensure that proceedings in the House are fair and orderly. Historically, the Speaker was very important, because he was a symbol of the independence of Parliament from the Crown. Even today, we accept the principle that the Speaker should be independent, and should act in the interests of the institution of Parliament, rather than the interests of the government or the governing party.

In practice this is difficult to achieve, however. The Speaker is elected as a Member of Parliament. Like all other Members, the Speaker represents voters in an electorate. Usually, the Speaker is a member of the government party and depends on that party for preselection for the next election. Many Speakers begin their term of office with good ideas of what they would like to do, but find it hard always to be independent, because of the political pressures on them.

Not all the work of Parliament is done by the Members acting together. More and more Australian Parliaments, like those elsewhere in the world, are using committees to examine Bills and other issues in greater detail and to report to the Parliament about them. Committees have many advantages. They are smaller and can make decisions more quickly. They can move around the country (or the State) to hear the views of voters directly. Importantly, committees have some success in breaking down strong disagreements or rigid divisions between Members from different parties. In a smaller group, people can get to know each other better, understand each other's points of view and feel more comfortable about saying what they really think so as to reach an agreed result.

One house or two?

Both the Commonwealth Parliament and all State Parliaments except Queensland also have two "Houses", which doubles the opportunity to vote yet again. Parliaments of this kind are called "bicameral" Parliaments which means that they have two "chambers" or Houses.

One House in each Parliament is a "popular" House, representing all the people equally. This is the House on whose support the government depends. In the Commonwealth Parliament it is called the House of Representatives. It will be considered in greater detail in the next chapter. The lower House of the State Parliament is called the Legislative Assembly in New South Wales, Victoria, Queensland and Western Australia and the House of Assembly in South Australia and Tasmania.

The second House in a bicameral Parliament is sometimes referred to as the "upper House". In the Commonwealth Parliament it is the Senate: see Chapter 11. The State upper Houses are all called the Legislative Council.

Parliaments have upper Houses for different reasons. Earlier, in less democratic times, upper Houses were elected by people who owned more property than others, to keep the lower Houses, elected by a wider range of voters, under control. That has changed now and voting qualifications are the same for both Houses. More recently, other reasons have developed for the use of an upper House. As we will see in Chapter 11, the Australian Senate was established to play a role in the federal system. Both the Senate and some of the State upper Houses now are valued as well for other reasons. Generally, proposed new laws, or Bills, must pass through or be voted on by both the upper House and the lower House. An upper House therefore provides the opportunity for a second look at these proposals. If an upper House is more independent of executive government than the lower House, it may be prepared to look at proposed laws and government action more carefully.

An upper House will not have much independence if most of its Members come from the government party. In this case, while new laws still must pass through two Houses, the upper House is likely to agree with the government. We sometimes describe a House of this kind as a "rubber stamp". On the other hand, an upper House which has a majority of

Opposition Members may disagree with the lower House just for the sake of it, which is equally unsatisfactory.

This suggests that an upper House should be elected quite differently from the lower House. And it is possible to experiment with different types of representation in an upper House, without the worries about forming a government which affect the choice of electoral system for lower Houses. Some Parliaments have taken this opportunity to elect the upper House through proportional representation, making it more likely that minor parties and independents will be elected. Proportional representation has been used for Senate elections since 1949. It is used for the Legislative Councils of New South Wales, Western Australia and South Australia as well.

A bicameral Parliament in which the lower House provides a base for the government and the upper House has Members who are independents or from minor parties has become very familiar in Australia. It solves some problems while creating others, however. In particular, it makes it quite likely that from time to time a very small number of upper House Members – perhaps only one – will decide whether government policies are put into effect or not. Proposals to abolish or reduce the power of upper Houses sometimes are made for this reason. They seem unlikely to be acceptable in the near future, however, unless a way can be found for lower Houses to take a more independent role.

Other elected representatives

So far, the discussion in this part has dealt only with the election of representatives to the Commonwealth and State Parliaments.

In fact, of course, Australians elect representatives for other purposes as well. Almost all of us live in a local government area and elect members to our local council. Indigenous Australians may also elect councillors to the Aboriginal and Torres Strait Islander Commission (ATSIC), which advises the executive government of the Commonwealth on indigenous matters and manages some government programs for the indigenous peoples.

Local government is set up under State legislation. It performs whatever jobs are given to it by the State and must act consistently with the legislation. ATSIC is established under Commonwealth legislation which, similarly, sets out what it can do.

Elected bodies of this kind create some tensions for the Australian system of government, which we have not yet worked out. Because they are elected, they have a different status than other bodies which are chosen or appointed by executive government and not elected by the people. The Australians who vote for them expect their representatives to have the chance to carry out the functions for which they were elected, as long as they follow the usual procedures for accountability to the voters.

On the other hand, these bodies also are established by other levels of government, which are seen to have responsibility for them and which have the legal power to become involved in various ways. In the case of local government, this sometimes takes the form of dismissing local councils or suspending elected local government altogether. To what extent should elected bodies of this kind be controlled by other levels of government, rather than left to the judgement of the voters themselves?

These tensions are related to the debate about whether local government should be included in the Australian Constitution. Local government already is recognised in (most) State Constitutions. This acknowledges the status of local government but does not give it much protection, because these parts of the State Constitutions are more easily changed than the Australian Constitution. The argument in favour of recognition of local government in the Constitution is that local government is important to Australian democracy. The argument against is that it would confuse responsibility for local government, between the Commonwealth and the States. A proposal to recognise local government in the Australian Constitution was put to referendum in 1988, but rejected. It may be discussed again, as Australia approaches the 100-year anniversary (centenary) of the Constitution in 2001.

10

The House of Representatives

What is the House of Representatives?

The House of Representatives is the lower House of the Commonwealth Parliament. It is designed to be the "popular" House, or the "House of the people". Because of this, it is the House from which the government is formed. After an election, the leader of the party with a majority of seats in the House of Representatives becomes Prime Minister. The Prime Minister is always a Member of the House of Representatives. A vote of support or "confidence" in the government in the House of Representatives brings on a new election or at least a change of government.

By contrast, the number of seats that a party holds in the Senate is not counted in deciding who will form government. Ministers who are Senators will not necessarily lose their jobs as Ministers if the Senate votes no confidence in them or in the government.

The design of the House of Representatives as the "people's House" makes it more important than the Senate in one other respect as well. There is a principle that has been around for a long time that the "people's representatives" should have control over taxing and spending. Under section 53 of the Constitution, Bills that deal with money therefore cannot begin in the Senate and most of these Bills cannot be amended by the Senate.

What does it mean to say that the House of Representatives is the "House of the people"? It must mean more than that its Members are elected, because Senators are elected too. It seems to suggest that there should be more of a direct link between the people and their elected representatives in this House. At the very least, by the standards of the 1990s, such a link requires that:

- The House of Representatives is elected by all adult Australian citizens.
- The House has enough Members to properly represent all Australians.
- In voting for this House, everyone's vote is equal (although there may be argument about what this means).
- Elections for the House of Representatives are held regularly and reasonably often, to be sure that its membership still reflects the preferences of the voters.

The rest of this chapter considers how the House of Representatives meets these conditions and the extent to which the Constitution provides a clear framework for them.

Elected by all Australians

The House of Representatives is set up by Part 3 of Chapter 1 of the Australian Constitution. The opening words of the first section in that part, section 24, are:

> The House of Representatives shall be composed of members directly chosen by the people of the Commonwealth ...

These words have proved to be extraordinarily important. They are as close as we get to a statement in the Constitution about who can vote for the House of Representatives. These days, the High Court might interpret them to mean that all adult Australian citizens are entitled to vote. As we will see in Chapter 13, the High Court has said that a real "choice" by the people in connection with this section of the Constitution requires freedom of political speech and communication, so that the "choice" is properly informed.

Otherwise, however, there is no right to vote directly stated in the Constitution. Section 41 looks a bit like such a statement. It says that no-one who has the right to vote at State elections can be prevented from voting in Commonwealth elections. In fact, however, that section applied only to rights to vote at the time of federation, and so no longer has any effect. In 1901, only South Australia and Western Australia had given the vote to women. Section 41 was intended to make sure that women from these States could vote in federal elections as well, whatever happened in the rest of the country.

Even if section 24 now means that all adult Australians can vote in elections for the House of Representatives, it certainly has not always been thought to mean that. Although women from all States were given the vote in federal elections in 1902, no-one thought that the Constitution required this to happen. Aboriginal Australians did not have a right to vote in federal elections until 1962. And voters in the Northern Territory and the Australian Capital Territory did not have the same voting rights as everyone else until 1974. Even now, representation for the Territories is set by the Commonwealth Parliament under section 122 of the Constitution and is not covered by section 24.

Depending on what the High Court might make of the opening words of section 24, the right to vote still depends largely on legislation rather than the Constitution itself. The relevant Act is the Commonwealth Electoral Act 1918. It gives the right (and requirement or obligation) to vote to all adult Australian citizens, with a few exceptions. British subjects who were on the electoral roll (the list of people who could vote) before 1984 are also entitled to vote. In fact, therefore, in 1997 the House of Representatives is elected by all adult Australians and by some others as well.

The number of Members

The Constitution sets the total number of Members of the House of Representatives (MHRs) for the States by reference to the number of Senators. The number of Senators is dealt with by section 7 of the Constitution which will be discussed in Chapter 11. Under section 24, the number of Members in the House is required to be "as nearly as practicable" twice the number of Senators. This is known as the "nexus" or connection between the two Houses. The Members and Senators for the Territories are not counted for this purpose.

There are presently 12 Senators for each State, or a total of 72. As long as this number of Senators continues, there will be at least 144 MHRs. This means that there is 1 MHR for every 80,000 Australian voters, more or less. It is a reasonable ratio, by the standards of other similar countries.

And, of course, the ratio is even better, if Senators and Members of State Parliaments are included.

This is not necessarily the most sensible way of deciding the total size of the House of Representatives, however. Ideally, the size of the House should be set from time to time at whatever level we consider necessary to properly represent the Australian people. This means, for example, that as the total population grows we should at least think about increasing the number of Members of the House of Representatives as well. In fact this has happened, because the size of the House has doubled since federation. But thanks to the nexus provision, the size of the Senate has doubled as well. In 1967 a proposal to amend the Constitution to break the nexus was passed by the Parliament, but it was rejected by the people of Australia in a referendum

The value of your vote

The central feature of an electoral system for a "people's House" is that everyone's vote is worth the same or, in other words, that every voter is treated as equal.

This would be easy to achieve, if we all voted for all Members of the House, using a system of proportional representation. For the reasons explained in Chapter 8, however, so far we have preferred to use an electoral system which is more likely to give one or other of the parties a clear majority in an election and so produce stable government. We elect our representatives from single Member electoral divisions and we use a system of preferential voting.

These arrangements are not required by the Constitution, although some sections assume that there are likely to be electoral divisions. According to section 24, the number of Members of the House of Representatives must be divided up at least between States. Under section 29, if there are no electoral divisions in a State the whole State must be used as a single electorate.

Think for a moment about the idea that voters are entitled to be treated equally and that everyone's vote should be worth the same. It would be possible to take this literally and to require each MHR to represent the same number of voters. In a system like ours which uses single Member electorates, this would mean that there should be approximately the same number of voters in each division. Would this be fair in electoral districts which are geographically very large, and more difficult to get around? It is sometimes argued that real equality of representation needs a smaller number of voters in electorates of this kind.

The Constitution provides rather mixed guidance on all this. The famous section 24 requires the number of Members chosen from each State to be "in proportion" to the number of the people of the State. The numbers must be checked every three years, in time for each general election. If one State gains population and another loses it, the number of MHRs will shift to reflect this change. There is no recognition here that large States like, say, Queensland or Western Australia should have more Members because of the distances to be travelled.

Beyond laying down a rule that no electorate should go across State borders, however, the Constitution says almost nothing about the principles on which electoral divisions are to be decided. Once again, the opening words of section 24 may be important. If there were huge differences in the numbers of voters in different electorates, it might not be possible to describe the House as "chosen by the people".

In practice, after a skirmish in the Parliament in the 1970s, electoral boundaries now are drawn regularly by an independent Electoral Commission in a way which ensures that the differences in numbers of voters is no more than 10 % above or below the average. What this means can be illustrated by the example in Chapter 8. If there were 10 electoral divisions and 1 million voters, the average in each division would be 100,000. Under the current law, it would be lawful for the number of voters in each division to range from 90,000 to 110,000.

There are two ways in which the Constitution clearly is different from the idea that everyone's vote is worth the same in elections for the House of Representatives.

One is the guarantee in section 24 that each State which joined the federation at the beginning (the "Original" States) will have at least 5 MHRs, whatever their population. Without this guarantee, only 3 or 4 MHRs would be elected from Tasmania, given the present size of its population.

The second departure from the principle is the possibility under section 25 that Australians of a particular race might not be counted in working out the number of MHRs to be elected from the State in which they live, if their State disqualified them from voting in State elections.

The purpose of the section was to discourage States from racial discrimination. To modern eyes, however, it makes matters worse. In fact, as you would hope, the States do not disqualify people from voting because of their race. Even if they wanted to do so, the Commonwealth's Racial Discrimination Act 1975 would now make any such State law invalid. It may be that section 25 should now be taken out of the Constitution and replaced by a statement forbidding racial discrimination, or giving a right to vote instead.

Regular elections

The Constitution requires elections for the House of Representatives to be held regularly and quite often. Under section 28, the maximum term of the House (period of time between elections) is three years. The House can be dissolved earlier than that by the Governor-General. A double dissolution of the House of Representatives and the Senate also is possible, in conditions described in Chapter 12.

Some people think that elections every three years is too often. It has clear advantages for democracy and accountability, particularly if there are limited opportunities for the community to contribute to government decision-making in between elections. But three years may not give governments enough time to plan and put difficult policies into effect before worrying about the next election. For these reasons, the terms of the lower Houses of most State Parliaments have been extended to four years in recent years.

If three years is too short, the position is made even worse by the fact that the House can be dissolved earlier by the Governor-General and an election held. In using this power, as with almost all others, the Governor-General acts on government advice. Even if the Prime Minister advised a very early election after, say, 18 months and had no good reason, a Governor-General could not refuse unless, perhaps, the Prime Minister had lost the support of the House. The result is that early elections have been very common. The average length of the House of Representatives in recent decades has been closer to two years than to three. It would be possible to improve this average simply by requiring the House to work its full term.

As we will see in the next chapter, elections for the House of Representatives are usually held at the same time as elections for half the Senate. This is convenient, and much less expensive that two elections would be. If the term of the House were lengthened, it would be necessary to change Senate terms too, if we wanted the elections to continue to be held at the same time.

One way of doing this would be to link the term of Senators to two terms of the House of Representatives, whatever that may be. This has been rejected several times, in referendums before. It might be more acceptable, however, if there were some guarantee that the House would not be dissolved early. Two States, Victoria and South Australia, presently have maximum four-year terms for the lower House of Parliament and "fixed" or minimum three-year terms. The House cannot be dissolved within the first three years unless, for example, the government has lost the support of the House. A solution of this kind might suit the Commonwealth Parliament as well.

11

The Senate

What is the Senate?

The Senate is the upper House of the Australian Parliament. It is an almost equal partner with the House of Representatives. Bills must pass both Houses, before they become law. Although Bills are usually decided on first in the House of Representatives and then in the Senate, they may be passed by the Senate first, if the Minister responsible for that part of government happens to be a Senator, rather than a Member of the House of Representatives.

For the reasons explained in Chapter 10, however, the House of Representatives has more power than the Senate over money Bills. The House of Representatives also is more important in choosing the executive government and keeping it in power.

Like the House of Representatives, the Senate is directly elected by all adult Australian citizens. In all other ways, however, the election system is different. The same number of Senators is elected from each State, even though there are differences in State populations. The original number of Senators from each State was six. At present it is 12. The mainland Territories have 2 Senators each.

Nor are the States divided into electorates for Senate elections. Instead, each of us votes for all the Senators to be chosen from the State in which we live. The voting system used in proportional representation. The result is that the major parties rarely have a majority of seats in the Senate and that the "balance of power" is held by minor parties or by independents.

Only some of this is in the Constitution. The Senate is set up by Part 2 of Chapter 1. The opening section of that part, section 7, requires there to be an equal number of Senators from each "original" State. It also says that each State shall form a single electorate for Senate elections "until the Parliament otherwise provides". It does not say anything about the voting system at all. It would be possible for the Parliament to completely change who is in the Senate by agreeing to a new voting system and/or dividing each State into Senate electorates. Governments occasionally threaten to do this, when the Senate blocks some of their Bills.

The differences in the way the Senate is elected are explained by the differences in the Senate's job, or the role they are meant to play. The framers of the Constitution designed the Senate as a State's House and a House of Review. What this means and how it works in practice are described in the rest of this chapter.

What is a States' House?

Without the Senate, it would not have been possible to persuade all six colonies to join the federation in 1901. At that time, most Australians lived in New South Wales and Victoria. If there had been only one House of Parliament, the Members from those two States would have outnumbered Members from all the other States and controlled national decision-making. So the framers of the Constitution decided to form a second House, to have an equal say in legislation, in which the people from each State would be represented equally. This was not a particularly new idea. The United States was a federation also, with an upper House called the Senate. The Australian Senate, very roughly, followed the United States model.

There are plenty of signs in the Constitution that the Senate was designed as a States House. The equal number of Senators from each State is the most obvious. In addition, however, the Constitution allows State Parliaments to decide the times and places of Senate elections and gives State Governors power to start the Senate election process ("issue the writs"). Section 15 requires State Parliaments to fill any vacancy in the Senate which takes place before the end of the term of one of the Senators for their State.

Most of these links with the States have become less important over time. Almost all Senators belong to a political party. They vote in the Senate with other Members from their party, not with other Senators from the same State. Senate elections are always held when the Commonwealth government suggests, through co-operation between the Commonwealth and the States. The Constitution was amended in 1977 to require States to fill a casual vacancy in the Senate with someone from the same party as the Senator who has left their job as Senator.

Does this mean that the Senate is not really a States House? Certainly, the Senate does very little to protect the interests of particular States or even of the States as a whole. But perhaps it was never likely that it would. The Senate is elected by the people of the States. It is not chosen by State governments as is, for example, the German upper House. The responsibilities of the Senate are nearly as broad as those of the House of Representatives.

When you think about it, it is not surprising that the Senate has a national rather than just a State focus. It could never have protected individual States – we rely on other parts of the Constitution to do that. It might have played a more important role in the federal system as a whole by, for example, taking a special interest in decisions about grants (money given by the federal government) to the States and intergovernmental agreements and treaties that relate to State power. However, even if it did this (and it might be a good idea) these are still only some of the national issues which the Senate must decide.

This does not mean that the Senate has nothing to do with the federal system. The original argument still applies: the Senate gives the people of the smaller States a greater voice in national decision-making than they would otherwise have had. It provides a larger group of Members from the smaller States, who can become Ministers or Members of parliamentary committees. People who have been in the Commonwealth Parliament say that Senators sometimes change policy in a way which helps their State by their discussions with other members of their political party or in Cabinet.

A House of Review

The idea that the Senate might be a House of Review was even less of a new idea. All colonial Parliaments had an upper House which acted as a check on the lower House. The House of Lords performed a similar function in the British Parliament.

The Australian Senate was different, however. All these other upper Houses were set up in a way which made them naturally more inclined to protect existing interests, because they represented people with power or money. But Senators were directly elected. And the qualifications for voters and candidates for Senate elections were the same as those for the House of Representatives. The majority in the Senate therefore shows the preferences of a majority of people in a majority of States at the time the elections were held.

What should a House of Review do? In many ways, we are still working this out. Most Australians would agree that it should not block the government in the lower House without good reason. Ideally, it should examine the strengths and weaknesses of legislation and look very carefully at government action while keeping in mind what is best for all. The need for the Senate to do these things has become more important as the party system has become stronger, making it less likely that the House of Representatives will act in this way.

The difficulty is, of course, that Senators belong to parties too. The Senate can carry out its review function better if neither of the major groups of parties has a majority in the Senate. And, generally, neither of them do, thanks to proportional representation. If the voting system were to change, however, the ability of the Senate to carry out a review function would be likely to change as well.

Even so, the system is open to criticism. Some objective standards have been developed, but not enough. Each Senator follows the policy, if any, of the party to which he or she belongs. A small number of Senators, representing a small number of voters can prevent a government from carrying out policies on which it was recently elected. Obviously, this may not be fair. On the other hand, it is one way of controlling the very strong power of a government with a majority in the House of Representatives between elections, which many think is a good idea.

The Senate and the Territories

As we have seen, the Constitution links the Senate closely with the States. But some Australians live in Territories, rather than in States. Should they be able to vote for the Senate too?

Whether they should or not, they can. In 1974, Commonwealth legislation provided for two Senators each from the Northern Territory and the Australian Capital Territory. The legislation was questioned in the High

Court, because section 7 says that "The Senate shall be composed of Senators for each State ...". The High Court did not agree with this argument. The judges said that under section 122 the Parliament had power to have Senators from the Territories. This section allows the representation of a Territory in either House in the way in which the Parliament thinks fit. The Territories have had Senators ever since. And this seems fair, particularly if the role of the Senate is to ensure better representation from all parts of the country in the Australian Parliament.

The Northern Territory raises another issue which affects the Senate. The Territory would like to become a new State in time for the constitutional centenary in 2001. As a new State, rather than an Original State, it would not be entitled to the same number of Senators. It also has a small population – but then, so does Tasmania. So how many Senators should a new State of the Northern Territory have? The same as the other States, so that everyone remains equal? Or a smaller number, at least until its population grows?

Terms of Senators

Members of the House of Representatives are elected for three years, or until the Governor-General dissolves the House. Again, Senators are different. Senators are elected for six years. Their terms are fixed. They begin on 1 July and run to 30 June six years later. The terms of Senators also are "staggered", which means that half the Senators stand for election every three years, while the other half remain in office. All of this can change if there is a double dissolution of Parliament to deal with a disagreement or a "deadlock" over a Bill between the Houses, which will be considered in Chapter 12.

A half Senate election may be held at any time in the 12-month period before the Senators' terms expire, but the new Senators will not take their seats until July. This flexibility usually enables half-Senate elections and elections for the House of Representatives to be held at the same time. One of the weaknesses of this system, however, is that laws continue to be passed by Senators who have not been re-elected while others who have been elected are not yet participating at all.

Longer terms and staggered elections are familiar in State upper Houses as well. Senators in the United States also have six-year terms, with one third of the Senate standing for election every two years. Some people feel that these arrangements help support the functions which the Senate is supposed to perform. It is less important for Senators to face elections frequently, because they do not determine who will be in government. It may be more important for Senators to be experienced and to be able to give more time to the work which the Senate is supposed to do.

As always, however, it is necessary to balance democracy and accountability of representatives, on the one hand, against the effectiveness of Parliament and executive government on the other. Generally, Australians seem to accept six-year terms for Senators. It would be more difficult to decide what to do if the term of the House of Representatives were extended to four years. One option would be to extend Senate terms to eight years, but this might be too long. At the other extreme, Senators might be given four-year terms, even though this might affect its work as a House of Review. This idea was put to referendum in 1988 and rejected. A third option mentioned in the last chapter would be to give Senators two terms of the House of Representatives. This has been rejected in the past as well, but it might be more acceptable if there were some guarantee that the House would not be dissolved early.

12

Disagreements between the Houses

When a disagreement becomes a deadlock

We say we have a deadlock in the Parliament when the House of Representatives passes a Bill, but the Senate refuses to pass it in a form which the House will agree to.

It is also possible, of course, for the Senate to pass a Bill which the House will not accept. We tend not to worry about this, however. If the House of Representatives passes a Bill, it means that the Bill also has the support of the government. Rejection by the Senate stops something which the government wants to do, to which a majority of the House has agreed. And, at least in principle, a majority of the House represents a majority of the people.

If the House of Representatives refuses to pass a Bill which the Senate has passed, the Bill simply fails. But if the Senate will not pass a Bill which comes to it from the House, our system assumes that something needs to be done to resolve the "deadlock".

Some deadlocks are different

To understand how the Constitution deals (or doesn't deal) with deadlocks, you need to understand the different kinds of disagreements that can occur over different types of Bills.

Deadlocks over Bills which authorise the executive government to spend money to meet its ordinary expenses are the most serious. Unless these Bills are passed quickly, the money which the executive can spend on, for example, family allowances, aged pensions and its own administration runs out. If that ever were to happen, government would simply come to a halt.

Deadlocks over other Bills may also be important, but the executive government can keep going. Delay in getting the Bill through the

Parliament may hold government up but will not stop it entirely. In many cases, it is possible for a compromise (an agreement part way between both views) to be agreed in the Senate and for the deadlock to be settled or resolved in this way.

There is one other type of Bill over which the Houses sometimes disagree, which is different again. Proposals to change the Constitution must be passed by Parliament before they are put to referendum. A deadlock in the Parliament over Bills of this kind prevents the Australian people voting on the proposal. One way of resolving the deadlock would be to put the Bill to referendum anyway, to see what the people think. If you look at section 128 of the Constitution, you will see that it seems to allow for this to happen. As we will see in Chapter 14, however, the section does not work like this in practice.

Why do deadlocks happen?

Disagreement between two different Houses of Parliament is unavoidable from time to time. The more similar the two Houses are to each other, the more likely they are to agree, of course. But if they are too similar, there is no point in having two Houses at all.

The House of Representatives and the Senate are very different in many respects. Their functions are different, whether you consider the Senate as a States' House or a House of review. And their membership is entirely different too. The House of Representatives represents the people in proportion to population. Its Members are chosen from individual electorates. The Senate represents all States equally, no matter how big or small the population. Senators are chosen by proportional representation by the people of each State, voting as a single electorate.

In addition to this, half the Senate is chosen at a different time from the House of Representatives. Senators have six-year terms, while those of MHRs last for three years, at most. Half the Senate usually is elected at the same time as the House of Representatives. The other half, however, is elected three years earlier, when the voters may have been in a different mood.

It is hardly surprising, then, that the two Houses sometimes disagree. And the situation becomes more complicated by the fact that most Senators are members of the same political parties which face each other in the House of Representatives. It is natural for Senators which come from the Opposition party or parties (the group not in power) to want to defeat some government proposals. They will be able to do so if they have a majority in the Senate or if they can get the independent Senators (those who do not belong to a party) or Senators from smaller parties to vote with them.

The differences in party numbers in the Senate and the House of Representatives are not only the result of differences in voting systems or in the timing of Senate elections. Some Australians choose to vote for different parties in the Senate and the House. This may be because they would like a particular party to be in government, but do not want the government to have too much power. In other words, they want the Senate to be a "check and balance" in the system of government. We consider checks and balances later, in Chapter 23, as one of the limits on government. The idea of the Senate as a check and balance is important to the way in which deadlocks are resolved.

How are deadlocks dealt with?

Section 57 of the Constitution describes a procedure or method for dealing with deadlocks.

The main step in the procedure is a dissolution of both Houses (or "double dissolution"), followed by an election. This is the only time when the whole Senate, instead of half the Senate, faces an election. The idea is that two completely new Houses are more likely to be able to reach agreement. An election also gives candidates a chance to find out what the voters think about the Bill which the Senate is refusing to pass.

There are several ways in which an election might resolve a deadlock. If the government changes, the House of Representatives might lose interest in the Bill because the particular people who supported the Bill will not have been re-elected. So the Bill will not be introduced again. If the same government is re-elected, it may have more support for the Bill in the Senate as well, and then the Bill may pass the Parliament in the ordinary way. But it is also possible, of course, that the Houses will not agree after the election and that the deadlock will continue.

In this case, one further step may be taken. A "joint sitting" may be held, in which both Houses meet and vote together on the Bill. If the Bill is passed by more than half of the total number of Members of both Houses, it can be given Royal Assent and become law. If not, that is the end of it.

These are very severe procedures, and section 57 of the Constitution is designed to ensure that there really is a deadlock before they are used. It requires the Senate to refuse to pass a Bill twice and for there to be three months between the time when the Senate fails to pass a Bill the first time and the House of Representatives passes it for the second time. If the Senate merely delays dealing with a Bill, instead of rejecting it outright, it may not be clear exactly when the three-month period started running. If there is a dispute about this, the High Court can decide.

Triggers for a double dissolution

There are a few odd features of section 57 which affect how it actually works.

One is that an election can be held at any time after a Bill has been rejected twice, until six months before the Constitution says an election has to be held. Another is that the section has been interpreted to allow disagreements over more than one Bill to be dealt with at the same time. Together, these features mean that Bills can be saved up during a term of Parliament to be used for a double dissolution if and when the government wants one. This is why the first Bill in each term of Parliament to be rejected by the Senate in accordance with section 57 is sometimes called a "trigger": it can be pulled at any time, like a trigger in a gun.

According to the Constitution, the key decisions under section 57 are made by the Governor-General. The Governor-General can dissolve the two Houses, after the Senate has rejected a Bill for the second time. The Governor-General can call a joint sitting, if the deadlock continues after an election. But the Governor-General acts on the advice of the government in exercising these powers, as he or she does in almost all others. In reality, then, the government decides whether a double dissolution will take place and whether a joint sitting will be held.

If a government wants an early election, a double dissolution is likely to be more attractive than a dissolution of the House of Representatives alone, as long as a "trigger" is available. A deadlock between the two Houses gives an excuse for an early election. A double dissolution also may give the government party a chance to win more Senate seats – perhaps even to win a majority in the Senate. If a double dissolution is possible, it therefore may be tempting to call one, whether the Bills which the Senate has rejected are important or not. There have been six double dissolutions since federation (in 1914, 1951, 1974, 1976, 1983, 1987). The arguments for and against the deadlocked Bills were not an election issue in any of them.

There has been a small (and quite proper) reaction by Governors-General to all of this. They always accept the advice which they are given under section 57. But in recent years they have asked governments to advise them on two extra points as well. Are the Bills important? And is the Parliament unworkable? The answers to these questions are then made public, to help voters themselves to judge whether it really was necessary to go to all the trouble of dissolving both Houses and having an early election.

Deadlocks over money

It takes a long time to resolve disagreements between the Houses through a double dissolution and joint sitting. The minimum period is at least six months. In most cases, it takes much longer. This means that section 57 is no use at all for dealing with deadlocks over Bills which authorise governments to spend money for "ordinary annual services" (that is, to keep the government running). A Bill of this kind is introduced every year at the time of the budget. It has to be passed before the last authorisation (or "appropriation") from the previous budget runs out. If it is not, one of two things will happen. The business of government will stop. Or the government will start spending money unlawfully.

There is nothing in the Constitution to deal with deadlocks like this. Mostly, we simply hope that they will not happen. In fact they have happened twice, in 1974 and 1975. On both of those occasions, by chance, however, it was possible to solve the deadlocks in another way.

It was possible because, as luck would have it, there were other Bills being considered at the time which had already satisfied section 57 and which offered a constitutional trigger. In 1974 there were six of these Bills.

When the Senate rejected the spending Bills, Prime Minister Whitlam therefore advised a double dissolution of both Houses, using these other six Bills to show that there was a deadlock within the meaning of the Constitution. He won the election. The Senate rejected the Bills again and the first (and, so far, the last) joint sitting in Australian history was held. The Bills were passed, although one of them later was considered invalid by the High Court. There had not been a period of three months between the time when the Senate "failed to pass" the Bill and the House passed it for the second time.

In 1975 there were 21 trigger Bills being discussed when the spending Bill was blocked in the Senate. This time, however, Prime Minister Whitlam did not want an election and he did not advise the Governor-General Sir John Kerr to dissolve the Houses. The result was one of the most debated actions in Australian constitutional history: the Governor-General's dismissal of a Prime Minister who still had the support of the House of Representatives. The leader of the Opposition, Malcolm Fraser, was made Prime Minister instead, on condition that he would advise the Governor-General to dissolve both Houses of the Parliament, using the 21 trigger Bills as the reason. In due course an election was held.

The odd sequel to this story is that the Prime Minister (Fraser) who advised the election on the basis of the 21 Bills over which the Houses were in disagreement won the election, with majorities in both Houses. However, the new Prime Minister did not resubmit the Bills to the Parliament. This is the most clear demonstration of all that section 57 can be used to call an election over Bills which are of no interest at all to the government.

It is possible, of course, that the Senate could reject key money Bills in circumstances where there are no trigger Bills available. If that were to happen, there would be no constitutional way of resolving the deadlock at all. Great strain would be placed on our institutions, including the position of Governor-General, and on our ability to follow the procedures of constitutional government.

Do we need to do anything about deadlocks?

The one type of disagreement between the two Houses which cannot wait until the next election is refusal by the Senate to pass the spending Bills which keep the government going. As we have seen, however, this is the one type of disagreement which we have no procedure to resolve. The deadlocks which can be resolved under the Constitution tend to be less important and the deadlock procedure tends to be used for other purposes instead.

There have been all sorts of suggestions for changing the Constitution to deal with deadlocks over key spending Bills. One is to not allow the Senate to reject these Bills. This would prevent a deadlock occurring at all. Another suggestion is to require a double dissolution as soon as the Senate rejects a key spending Bill for the first time. This would resolve the deadlock quickly.

These options were discussed quite a lot in the years following the dismissal of the government in 1975. Interest in the issue has since died down, however. We have begun to assume that it could not happen again.

The issue might come up again in the course of debate over whether Australia should no longer have the Queen as Head of State and, in that sense, became a "republic". If this were to happen, we would need to provide an Australian Head of State. Some options would require the Constitution too state more clearly what the Head of State can do. This might mean that we would have to decide whether the Head of State should play a role in settling deadlocks over money Bills and, if so, what that role should be.

13
Democratic rights

The other side of the fence

In a democracy, most of the governing is done through representatives of the people. This is why Constitutions spend a lot of time describing representative institutions: how they are set up, what they can do, their relationships to each other.

The Australian Constitution is no exception, as we have seen in the past few chapters. But this chapter considers the rules from the other side of the constitutional fence. Government will not be representative unless it has some relationship with the people. It will not be democratic unless it is chosen by the people, in some acceptable way. Representative democracy needs people, as well as representatives. Which brings us to democratic rights.

What are democratic rights?

Democratic rights are the rights which each community considers necessary to make its democratic arrangements work. Different communities may have different views about this. But in Australia and in other Western democracies it is possible to identify at least a core of rights without which we would not accept that government was really democratic.

The most obvious are the rights to vote and to stand for Parliament or for any other elected office. Connected with both of them, however, is a third right – a right to equality. This helps to decide who should have the other two rights. If we did not accept that people were equal, we might give the vote to some members of the community and not to others. Equality means that everyone should be able to vote and that everyone's vote should be worth the same.

This does not mean "everyone" literally. We can agree that it is okay to limit the right to vote to people who are full members of our community; in other words, to those who are "citizens". We can justify keeping these rights away from people who cannot exercise them because, for example, they are too young. The standards must be objective, however, and go along with the most common views about what democracy is.

There are other democratic rights as well. People need to know what their representatives have done, are doing and are proposing to do, in order to decide who to vote for. People need to be able to talk to each other about these matters and to talk to their representatives. They need to be able to march in the streets or to hold a demonstration outside Parliament House or to protest in some other way, if they are really annoyed at what is going on and can't get much help by speaking to their representatives alone. They need to be able to form new political parties or to join together in other groups, to try to influence government for the future.

None of these rights is unlimited or can be exercised without considering other people, of course. We need to balance the right of some people to march and to protest against the right of others to go about their business in the normal way. Political parties need to be registered, to ensure that they are real. The right to freedom of speech must be exercised in a way which does not cause harm to others. There will always be limits on the rights of individuals in a community. Where those limits lie is an important (and often controversial) question. But the rights are important too. They make our democracy work.

How should democratic rights be protected?

Rights can be protected in many different ways. Most countries use a mixture of all of them.

Many rights are recognised by the common law. This is the law developed by judges, through their decisions in cases, over the centuries in Britain and later in Australia. Freedom of speech and association, and the rights to assemble and to protest are recognised by the common law. Common law rights must be respected by executive governments. They can be taken away by Parliaments, however.

The role of Parliament in relation to rights therefore is important. Parliament can protect rights in a negative way, by stopping itself from overruling rights which are recognised by the common law. And Parliament will sometimes create new rights, through legislation. The rights to vote and to stand for election, for example, did not exist at common law and had to be created.

Rights can also be protected by putting them into a Constitution. If the Constitution has a special status (and most Constitutions do) this will prevent Parliament overriding the rights in the Constitution, accidentally or on purpose. It will not necessarily prevent Parliament placing some limits on rights for the good of the community as a whole, however. Different countries describe these limits differently. As an example, the South African Constitution allows limits "of general application" to be placed on rights if they are "reasonable and justifiable in an open and democratic society based on dignity, equality and freedom ...". In other words, the Parliament can place limits on rights, in the interests of the whole community, as long as the limits meet these standards.

In this chapter, we are concerned only with democratic rights. Chapter 25 deals with rights more generally. As we will see there, Australia tends to rely on the common law and Parliaments to protect rights. As a result, there is very little protection for the rights of individuals in the Constitution.

In Australia, we assume that we can rely on Parliament to protect rights generally because Parliament is democratically elected. In other words, we assume that Parliament would not ignore rights or treat individuals or groups badly. Parliament represents us. Each of the Members of Parliament wants to be re-elected. But this makes it all the more important to make sure that democracy itself is protected. And we may not be able to rely on Parliament to protect democratic rights. For example, the group which presently has a majority in Parliament could be tempted to try to stay in government by changing the voting rules to give itself an advantage. For these reasons, there may be better arguments for protecting democratic rights in a Constitution than there are for protecting others.

How does Australia protect democratic rights?

There is no clear protection of democratic rights in the Australian Constitution at all. As we have already seen, there is no specific right to vote. Section 41 guarantees that everyone who could vote in State elections at the time of federation could vote in federal elections as well, but there is nobody still alive to take advantage of this. There is no right to stand for Parliament (although there is a list of reasons why someone cannot stand for election). There are no express statements of rights to freedom of speech, or protest, or association.

Mostly, of course, Australians have these rights. They come from Acts of Parliament or the common law, however, not from the Constitution. This means that any of them can be changed by another Act of Parliament. One of the reasons why these rights were not included in the Constitution is that there was no status of Australian citizen at the time of federation and no agreement about equality. But we have both now.

Some democratic rights can probably be seen to exist or implied from other provisions of the Constitution, and in particular from those dealing with Parliament. Think again, for example, about the opening words of section 24, "The House of Representatives shall be directly chosen by the people of the Commonwealth ...". It is not hard to see that these words could be understood to require all the "people of the Commonwealth" to be entitled to vote, unless there is a good reason for not allowing them. It is possible that these words might be understood to require some equality in the value of each person's vote, although the High Court has not accepted this argument.

The High Court has said, however, that the requirement for the people to "choose" their Members of Parliament in this part of the Constitution requires "freedom of political communication". The argument is that Australians cannot make a "choice" that they really understand unless they have information about what candidates stand for and are free to state their political views openly and to talk about political issues amongst themselves. It is possible that the same kind of argument could be used to give constitutional protection for other democratic rights. There is a limit to which rights can or should be implied in this way, however.

While the Constitution does not give a right to stand for Parliament, section 44 lists some conditions which will disqualify or stop Australians from standing for the Commonwealth Parliament or from being a Member of it. Two of these, in particular, have caused trouble from time to time. One is section 44(1) which disqualifies Australians who also are citizens of another country from standing for Parliament. There are very many Australians who hold dual citizenship lawfully.

The second troublesome disqualification applies to people who hold an "office of profit under the Crown" under section 44(4). Anyone employed in any way by the Commonwealth or a State or Territory government is covered by this section. Obviously, once someone has been elected to Parliament, they should not still be employed by government (or by anyone else). But it seems unfair to require them to quit their jobs before they run for Parliament. After all, they might not win.

Democratic rights and the States

The Australian Constitution deals mainly with the Commonwealth institutions of government: the Commonwealth Parliament; the Commonwealth executive government; the Governor-General; the federal courts. It does not say much about State governments, although it mentions them from time to time. Mostly, how State and Territory governments work is left to the Constitutions of each of the States and to the Self-Government Acts of the Territories.

There are two exceptions to this, which concern democratic rights.

One was mentioned before, in Chapter 10. Section 25 recognises that State Parliaments might prevent some of their own people from voting in State elections, because of their race. In fact, the section tries to stop this from happening, by saying that these disqualified groups would not be counted for Commonwealth purposes either, when the number of Members of the House of Representatives which a State should have was being worked out. In other words, this part of the Constitution is trying to influence laws about State elections but, at least to modern eyes, in a very strange way. A more direct approach would be to give all adult Australians the right to vote in Commonwealth and State elections or to stop discrimination because of race.

The second exception has to do with freedom of political communication again. As we have seen, the High Court has said that Australians must be free to communicate on political matters if the Commonwealth Parliament is genuinely to be "chosen by the people". The Commonwealth Parliament cannot take this freedom away, beyond acceptable limits. But what does this say about State Parliaments, or about freedom of political speech about State political matters? Most probably, State Parliaments could not limit the freedom either, if this would prevent Australians talking freely about national political issues. For example, no State could pass a law to prevent extreme political parties putting forward their views, because that would affect the Commonwealth Parliament as well. What is not clear at present, however, is whether the guarantee in the Australian Constitution applies to all political communication, whether Commonwealth or State. It may not be possible to draw neat lines between the Commonwealth and the States where political communication is concerned.

A question for the future is whether the Australian Constitution should protect the essentials of democracy at the State as well as Commonwealth levels. Federalism is supposed to improve and spread democracy. To do this, State governments must act democratically too. The argument against national constitutional protection of this kind is that State communities should be able to choose and change their own democratic institutions. Choosing and experimenting with different methods are values of federalism too. All of this is of course true. The only issue is whether the national Constitution should set the basic guidelines for everyone.

14

Changing the Constitution

A direct say for people

One area of national decision-making in which people have a direct say is in changing the Constitution.

In section 128, all changes to the wording of the Constitution must be passed by the Commonwealth Parliament and put to a vote of the people, at a "referendum". To pass at referendum, a proposal must be approved by a majority of voters in all States and Territories. It must also be approved by a majority of voters in a majority of States: in other words, in at least four of the six States.

There are a few proposals for change which need to be approved by voters in States affected by the proposal as well. For example, this would be necessary for a proposal which would change the rule that the Original States have an equal number of Senators, or which changed the sections of the Constitution dealing with State boundaries. It probably is necessary for a proposal which changes section 128 itself. In practice, if a change is one which requires the approval of people in the States affected, it is likely to require approval in all States.

If democratic government draws its authority from the people and if the Constitution gives the framework for democratic government it is not at all surprising that the Constitution requires the agreement of the people before it is changed. Nevertheless, use of the referendum in this way is still not that common. Even in the 1990s, only about 20 percent of countries use the referendum for constitutional change. In the 1890s, when the Constitution was written, it was even more unusual.

Parliament acts first

A proposal to change the Constitution must be passed first by the Commonwealth Parliament, before it is put to referendum.

This gives the Parliament (and therefore the government) control over the proposals on which people can vote. This kind of referendum is sometimes called "passive", because the people do not choose the issues to vote on, but vote on whatever is put to them. It gets rid of the difficulties that sometimes come with the "popular initiative" where the people themselves can put proposals to referendum. It helps avoid the danger that groups who have one particular issue they care about will use the referendum to try to get support for proposals which would not be for the good of the whole community. It prevents things being put into the Constitution which should not be there at all.

There is a down side as well, however, with this system. The requirement for the Parliament to pass proposals for constitutional change before they are put to referendum limits the kind of proposals which are likely to be put. The Parliament would probably not put proposals which would limit its own power, for example. The need for the Parliament to act first also encourages the government and the opposition parties to look at proposals for constitutional change in the same way they would treat any other Bill which came before the Parliament. In this way, the Constitution and changes to it sometime become more of an issue between the parties than is necessary.

It might be a good idea to have another way of putting proposals to referendum as well, if we could think of one which was suitable. The popular initiative is one option. Another is to allow a proportion of State Parliaments (say, four) to introduce proposals for change. Different people have different views on both of these suggestions but neither seems to have support among a large number of people.

Alternatively, the Commonwealth Parliament might find ways to consider a wider variety of options for constitutional change and to develop them in a less party political way. It might, for example, set up a parliamentary committee on the Constitution and require it to hold public meetings from time to time. Or the Parliament might establish a constitutional convention every so often (say, every 20 years) and agree to follow its advice.

There is room for some flexibility even under present arrangements. Obviously, the two Houses of Parliament may disagree over proposals for constitutional change, just as they disagree over other Bills. The framers of the Constitution recognised, however, that this type of deadlock is different, because the people themselves are available to settle it. Section 128 therefore says that if one House passes a referendum Bill which is rejected by the other and if the first House passes the Bill again after three months, the Governor-General may put it to referendum. In other words, if one House of Parliament is prepared to pass a proposal in this way, it should be put to the people to decide.

In practice, it does not work like this, however. If a Bill passes the House of Representatives twice it may be put to referendum, and this has sometimes happened. Experience shows, however, that a Bill which is passed twice by the Senate and rejected by the House will not be put to referendum at all. The reason is that in this as in other matters the Governor-General acts on executive government advice. A government which has voted against a Bill in the House of Representatives will not advise the Governor-General to put it to referendum. Governments could adopt a different practice on this, however, if they chose to do so.

Can the Constitution be changed in any other way?

The Constitution itself can be changed only by referendum. But the way it works can be changed in various ways.

Some sections of the Constitution set out a rule which was meant to be used only until Parliament passed a law which said something different. These sections include the words "until the Parliament otherwise provides …". There are a lot of them. In most cases, the Parliament has "provided otherwise" (passed laws or Acts) and those sections of the Constitution are being used no longer. The rule in section 7 that each State votes for its Senators as a single electorate has not been changed by the Parliament, however. If it were changed, it would greatly affect the way in which the Senate works.

As we will see in Chapter 20, the Constitution divides power between the Commonwealth and the States by listing all the Commonwealth's powers in section 51. But it also lets the Commonwealth make laws on other matters when they are "referred" to it by a State (the State Parliament asks the Commonwealth to make the law). Under one of these references, for example, the Commonwealth can make laws about children whose parents are not married, to broaden the scope of the Family Law Act. References of power by the States to the Commonwealth therefore can change the division of power laid down by the Constitution itself.

Other forms of co-operation between the Commonwealth and the States have a similar effect. For example, the Constitution allows the States to set up or impose income tax, but they don't. The Commonwealth imposes all the income tax, and gives money or makes grants to the States instead. The Constitution does not give the Commonwealth power over universities, but it actually does have this power, by providing a lot of the money for universities. The Constitution does not let the Commonwealth control the way in which people form companies, but there is a national corporations law, which is very like a Commonwealth law and which works in the same way. The Constitution gives the States power to decide the times and places of Senate elections, but in practice those elections are held when and where the Commonwealth wants.

How the Constitution works can also be changed through decisions by judges. For example, section 92 says that interstate trade shall be "absolutely free". What can that possibly mean? Certainly it cannot mean that people can do whatever they like in interstate trade, including sell illegal guns or drugs, or carry diseased plants or animals from one part of the country to another. To make the section work, it has been necessary for the High Court to explain what it means. There have been several different explanations over the years. But in 1988, the High Court said that the section stops the protection of the trade of one State against competition from another. This is probably more or less what the framers of the Constitution meant when they wrote section 92.

These ways of changing the effect of the Constitution are all important. They can only be used in certain situations, however. If we want to change the way the Constitution works in a major way it is best to change the words of the Constitution, through referendum. Many changes could only be made in that way. For example, it would not be possible to make the term of the House of Representatives longer or to give Australians with dual citizenship the right to stand for Parliament without a referendum.

Voting in a referendum

When you vote in a referendum, you are actually voting to accept or reject the Bill to change the Constitution. The Bill sets out the wording of the changes to be made. They may include taking things out of the Constitution, or adding to it.

The rules are the same as for elections. Voting is compulsory (you have to do it). You need to go to a polling booth to vote. A referendum usually (but not always) takes place separately from an election, to try to make the main parties support it. This is an expensive way of holding referendums. If we could work out other ways of encouraging the parties to agree on decisions about the Constitution, a vote on a referendum could be held at the same time as an election, and would not cost much more at all.

One problem with referendums to change the Constitution is helping voters to understand the issues. Many Australians do not know a lot about the Constitution. It has not been taught in a clear way in schools for a long time. People who move to Australia are not told much about it either. It is hard for people to understand a suggestion to change the Constitution, in these circumstances.

It is made harder still by the official information given to voters. Under Commonwealth law, Members of Parliament who voted for and against a Bill to change the Constitution are each allowed to write the arguments for and against the Bill, to be given to voters. In other words, in referendums like in the courts and in the Parliament itself, we think that a contest between two sides will produce the best result. Use of the "yes/no" cases is fair, in the sense that it gives each side in the Parliament its say. But it does not necessarily help the voters, who must decide the issue. It might be better to provide a method of giving voters more factual information instead, or as well. For example, when New Zealand holds a popular vote an independent committee gives out information to help people to understand what the issues are.

The record of referendums

Forty-two proposals to change the Constitution have been put to referendum since federation. Thirty-four have been rejected. Eight have passed.

We tend to think of this as a very bad record. But, in fact, it is not as bad as all that. Some of the referendums which have been passed have been important. For example, one gave the Commonwealth power over social services (like hospital benefits). Another allowed Australians in some Territories to vote in referendums. Almost all these referendums have come up when there clearly was a problem with the Constitution which people could understand and accept. And all passed very easily, with majorities in all or nearly all States as well as with national majorities. Most popular was the referendum to remove discrimination against the Aboriginal people, which had more than 90% support across Australia.

There are all sorts of theories about why the other proposals failed. In some cases the answer may be the obvious one: the proposals were not very good, or the voters simply did not like them. No doubt there are other reasons as well. Referendums are too often a political party issue. There is very little public discussion before proposals are put to referendum. Voters do not always understand what proposals mean and it is hard for them to find out.

With this history, the idea of holding an elected Convention to consider a republic in February 1998 is an interesting one. A Convention gives people a chance to have a say before the question that will be in the referendum is decided. It breaks down the usual differences between parties. It should help people to understand the issues, long before a referendum takes place. We might think about using conventions again in the future, depending on how this one goes.

15

Different kinds of decisions

Three kinds of decisions

There are three main kinds of decisions made under a system of government like ours. Legislative decisions make new law. Judicial decisions settle disputes by applying the law. Executive decisions cover everything else.

Why does this matter? For two reasons, at least. The first is that different kinds of decisions are made by different parts of government. Legislative decisions generally are made by Parliament. Judicial decisions should only be made by courts. Executive decisions are made somewhere within executive government. As we will see in Chapter 18, there are many different "executive" bodies to make them.

It makes sense, then, that different kinds of decisions are changed in different ways as well. If you disagree with an executive decision, you probably can go to a court if you think it is unlawful, or to a tribunal or an ombudsman if you think it is wrong for other reasons. (An Ombudsman is an independent person appointed to deal with complaints about government.) If you disagree with a judicial decision, you may be able to go to or appeal to a higher court. A law made by Parliament can only be changed by Parliament itself, however, unless a court says that it goes against the Constitution.

What is a legislative decision?

A legislative decision is one which makes new law. Law provides a binding rule about what people must or must not do. Law has the power of the state behind it, which means that it must be obeyed.

Any decision which changes your legal rights or places duties on you is a legislative decision. For example, it is not lawful at present to smoke marijuana. A decision to make it lawful would be a legislative decision.

Shops in Victoria used to be closed on Sundays. Now they can open if they want to. Only a legislative decision could require us to pay a new tax (say, a GST), or make it illegal to fish without a licence, or allow the government to take people's property for a new airport, or a road.

Generally, law is made by a Parliament. There are two exceptions, however. One is that Parliament can give its legislative power to executive government. This happens quite a lot although, in principle, only less important legislative decisions should be made in this way.

Secondly, within limits, the decisions of courts also make law. This is because decisions of courts must be followed by later courts and in this way become "binding" (must be followed). And while the main job of the courts is to find and apply existing law, very often the law is not clear. When this happens, the decision of the court will have "made" new law.

What is a judicial decision?

Judicial decisions settle disputes according to law. Decisions about who should pay damages for a car accident; or whether a Member of Parliament has been defamed or spoken badly of by a newspaper article; or whether it is legal to deport a drug dealer; or whether native title exists on land over which there are pastoral leases are all judicial in character.

Where does the law come from, which the courts apply?

These days, much of it comes from legislation. The most important legislation is made by the Commonwealth or State or Territory Parliaments and is called Acts of Parliament, or statutes. Legislation which is made by executive government with the authority "delegated" to it by Parliament may be called regulations or statutory rules (or lots of other things). Local government sometimes makes delegated legislation as well, called "by-laws".

The common law is another source of Australian law. Kinds of law which still rely a lot on the common law include criminal law, contract law and civil liberties law.

The third source of law is the Constitution itself. This is different to the others. It is our most fundamental or basic law. All other laws must agree with it.

What is an executive decision?

Executive decisions put decisions of Parliament and the courts into effect ("execute" them) and generally make the system of government work. Section 61 of the Constitution says that executive power "extends to the execution and maintenance of this Constitution and of the laws of the Commonwealth". It is easiest to think of an executive decision as anything which is not legislative or judicial. Executive decisions are important, because they often affect people in their everyday lives. Decisions about whether you are entitled to Austudy, or whether you will get a tax refund or whether your aunt can get a visa to visit Australia are all "executive" decisions.

The government gets a lot of its power to make executive decisions from legislation. Parliaments make laws, but they cannot predict all the different situations to which the laws must apply. To cope with this, a law often gives the executive government "discretion" or the ability to decide what should happen in different situations.

For example, under the Australian Citizenship Act the Minister may give Australian citizenship to people who meet residency and other requirements and who are "of good character". It is not possible for Parliament to spell out in legislation exactly what "good character" means. Parliament must leave a decision of this kind to a Minister, or to whoever else is putting the Act into effect.

Executive government does not rely on Parliament for all its power to make decisions, however. The executive government has some power of its own, as well. The government can do all sorts of things which any ordinary person can do: make contracts; buy land; buy and sell shares. The executive government does not need Parliament's approval to run a government bookshop; or to buy new computers; or to sell all the government cars. Parliament could pass a law to control how the executive does these things, however. If it did, the executive government would have to obey.

Some other powers of the executive government are special, because they are the kinds of power that only this branch of government has. Sometimes they are called "prerogative" powers, because they once were important powers exercised by the King or Queen. Decisions to make binding agreements, or treaties, with other countries are executive decisions of this kind. So are decisions to declare war, or make peace, or grant mercy to someone who has been found guilty of an offence. These decisions can be made without Parliament's express approval also, unless Parliament decides otherwise.

Why have these differences?

There is nothing very new and different about dividing power to make decisions between different parts of government. Most systems of government have a "separation of powers". It is one way of preventing government becoming too powerful. We will look at it again, in Chapter 24.

Other organisations divide power between different people and bodies too. A social club, for example, may give some powers to a Board of Management, some to an executive committee, some to a general meeting of the members, and so on. The aim is to work out which part of the organisation can best perform which functions. The executive committee is likely to develop a plan for the year to put to the Board. It may also make routine decisions. More important decisions usually will be made by the whole Board. Really important decisions will probably be left to the members as a whole.

And so it is with government. Parliament, the executive government and the courts each operate differently. Once again, the trick is to match the right decisions to the right body. Parliament is directly elected. It meets in public. It is made up of different Members, with different views. It is set up to make the most important decisions, which change the law, or impose taxes, or authorise the government to spend money. There may be some other important decisions which Parliament does not presently make, but should. Decisions about whether Australia should agree to an international treaty are a possible example.

For the same reasons, however, Parliament should not be expected to make decisions which are urgent, or which need to be kept confidential. Parliament cannot move quickly, if a lot of decisions need to be made at once. Parliament is too big to develop major new policies. Executive government is better at making decisions of these kinds. It has a small number of Ministers in Cabinet at its head and a large number of public servants and other agencies or offices who can carry out their directions.

And, similarly, the courts are better able to settle legal disputes than either Parliaments or governments. Judges are expert in the law. Courts are independent, and have procedures to make sure that parties are treated fairly. Courts hear the parties' arguments in public, so that other people can see that the courts are fair too. And courts give reasons for their decisions, so that the person who lost can understand why.

Finally, in Australia, there is one decision which no part of the government can make. That is the decision to change the Constitution. That decision is so important that we believe it must be approved by the Australian voters too.

16

Government and Parliament

Where does a government come from?

Parliament is elected by the people. Courts, as we will see, are chosen by executive governments. And governments are drawn from Parliaments, under a system often called "responsible government". Countries which use this system do not necessarily have governments which are more "responsible" than countries which don't. Responsible government gets its name because the executive government is supposed to be responsible to the Parliament for what it does and how it does it.

All Australian governments are chosen under a system of responsible government. The rules are much the same everywhere. This book is concerned mainly with the Australian Constitution, however, and this chapter deals mainly with the Commonwealth government and Parliament.

Having Parliament's confidence

The main rule of responsible government is that the government is chosen because it has the support of the lower House of Parliament. It usually stays in office as long as it keeps this support.

For the Commonwealth government, having "the confidence of the House" means that a majority of Members of the House of Representatives will support the government when it needs it. This will happen automatically if, as is usual, a majority of Members of the House belong to the government party or parties. It is possible to have a government whose members are not in a majority, however, as long as enough independent Members or Members from smaller parties are prepared to vote with the government on important matters.

This is the way this actually works. After an election, we count the number of seats each party has won, to see who has a majority. This usually is obvious on election night but, if an election is close, it may take a bit longer. Once the result is clear, the Governor-General invites the leader of the winning party to be Prime Minister and to "form a government". In doing this, the Governor-General usually acts on the advice of the last Prime Minister although sometimes he (or, maybe one day, she) exercises an independent discretion. The other Ministers then are appointed by the Governor-General on the advice of the new Prime Minister.

Choosing a Prime Minister in this way really involves guessing who Parliament will support. The guess is almost always right, because the party system makes it easy to predict. It would be possible to leave the decision to Parliament itself, however. This would mean calling Parliament together as soon as possible after an election and asking it to pass a positive vote of confidence in someone. This happens, for example, in South Africa and in Germany.

Once a government is formed, it stays in office until the next election, unless the House loses confidence in it. This is not very likely, where the government's own supporters have a majority. But if it happened, the government would need either to resign or to convince the Governor-General to call an early election.

How do we know when a government has lost the confidence of the House? It will be obvious if the House passes a vote of "no confidence" in the government. It is almost as obvious if the House refuses to pass the main budget Bills, because governments cannot continue without money. If a government loses other votes, however, there may be an argument about whether it has lost the confidence of the House or not. In Australia, governments are so used to winning every vote that any loss tends to be treated as an issue of confidence.

A government remains in office until a new government is chosen after an election. But as soon as it is decided to have an election, the government becomes a "caretaker". It is not supposed to put new policies into operation or to make new appointments during this time, at least without discussing it with the opposition. Everything is supposed to go on hold until the election is over.

Being responsible

The executive government depends on the confidence of the House of Representatives. In turn, the executive government is responsible to Parliament. What this means in practice is not clearly defined. But there are certain standard ways in which responsibility is demonstrated.

Each Minister is responsible for specific areas of government, which sometimes are called his or her "portfolio". Ministers must answer questions in Parliament on the areas for which they are responsible. They must explain to Parliament the meaning and purpose of new laws which they ask Parliament to pass. Sometimes they make statements to Parliament about major new policies. They may be called before parliamentary committees, to answer more questions.

Even so, it is hard for the House of Representatives to really *make* government responsible to it. Government Members probably won't want to show the government up in public, and they are usually in a majority. Ministers will often be able to get away with giving vague answers to questions or refusing to provide information at all. Even when a serious mistake is made, government Members probably won't support a vote of no confidence against the government as a whole, or even against a Minister.

The House is still important in the day-to-day working of responsible government, however. Parliament meets in public and the opposition has a say, quite often a very important say. For example, if an issue is serious enough and a combination of the opposition in Parliament and the media and public outside disagree with government policy, this may cause a government to change its policies or a Minister to resign.

What makes all this work?

You will not find much of this in the Constitution. The chapter that deals with it is Chapter 2, which is called *The Executive Government*. It has only 9 sections, half of which are no longer important. It does not mention the Prime Minister or responsible government or the responsibility of the government to Parliament.

The closest we come to a reference to these matters is section 64. This section refers to "officers" who "administer the Departments of State" and who will be the "Queen's Ministers of State". They must be Members of Parliament, at least within three months after appointment. They are advisers to the Governor-General and they hold office during his "pleasure".

What makes the Governor-General choose Ministers who have the confidence of Parliament? What stops the Governor-General getting rid of Ministers who no longer please him (or her)? In both cases, the answer is that Parliament controls the money. No government can demand taxation or spend money without Parliament's approval. The Governor-General must choose Ministers with the confidence of the House of Representatives in order to keep the business of government going. While the Constitution appears to give the Governor-General a free choice, in practice there is almost no choice at all.

Money and Parliament

Even though it is very important, there is not much in the Constitution about Parliament's control of money either.

There is no doubt that Parliament must approve taxation, but the Constitution does not actually say so. The rule comes originally from the common law and from the British Bill of Rights of 1689. This is now part of Australian law. It was taken for granted by the framers of the Constitution and we take it for granted now.

The Constitution is a little more clear about spending. Under section 81, all money which the Commonwealth raises must be paid to one central fund, called the Consolidated Revenue Fund. It cannot be spent without the authority of Parliament, which is called an "appropriation". If Parliament does not appropriate the money it is unlawful to spend it. It would be possible to go to a court to have unlawful spending stopped.

The main Appropriation Bills are put to Parliament every year, at the time of the budget. If the House of Representatives rejected them, it would bring the government down. But there is nothing in the Constitution to say that Parliament can appropriate money for general government expenses for only one year. Reading the Constitution word for word, it seems that it would be possible for a new government to persuade Parliament to appropriate enough money to cover its entire three-year term. Even if a government did this, however, it could not prevent Parliament being called together for that time. Under section 6, Parliament must meet at least once a year – as, indeed, you would hope.

How does the Senate fit in?

As you can see, the main rules of responsible government deal with the House of Representatives.

When we say that government must have the confidence of Parliament, we really mean the House of Representatives. After an election, we count the numbers in the House to decide who the government will be. And in normal times, the support of the House ensures that a government stays in office.

In Australia, however, the rules of responsible government must also take the Senate into account. The government is responsible to the whole Parliament, including the Senate. Ministers may be Members of either House. Ministers who are Senators must answer questions in the Senate. They introduce Bills in the Senate and appear before Senate committees. The Senate has the same rights to government information as the House. In one sense, the Senate is more effective than the House in making the government responsible to Parliament.

There is some conflict, however, between the function of the Senate and the idea that the government depends on the confidence of the lower, more popularly elected House. The Senate has the same power as the House of Representatives to reject money Bills. The government does not depend on the confidence of the Senate. But if the Senate will not approve the appropriation of funds, in practice, the government cannot keep going.

This happened in 1975, when the Senate refused to pass key money Bills. Prime Minister Whitlam refused to resign. The Ministers were dismissed by Governor-General Kerr. So, the action of the Senate forced a government out of office, even though it still had the confidence of the House of Representatives.

The leader of the opposition, Mr Fraser, was appointed as "caretaker" Prime Minister until an election could be held. He did not have the support of the House, which passed votes of no confidence in him. This did not make government impossible as it would normally have done, however. The Appropriation Bills already had been passed by the Senate, so money was legally available. And an election was called immediately, which the Fraser government won.

17

The Head of State

Who is the Head of State?

The Head of State is the person who, literally, is at the top of the system of government. In countries like the United States and South Africa the Head of State also leads the government. In others there is a separate Head of State. Australia is one of these.

These days Queen Elizabeth II is the Australian Head of State. That is why she is called the Queen of Australia. She is also, however, Queen of many other countries which once were British colonies. Even when they were colonies it was obvious that one person could not carry out the functions of Head of State in all colonies at the same time. And so the Crown was represented in each of its "realms" (or places it ruled) (except for the United Kingdom itself) by someone else who, usually, was called a Governor-General.

As the colonies became independent the position of Governor-General became more important and that of the monarch less important. Australia was no different. In 1975, for example, the Speaker of the House of Representatives complained to the Queen when Governor-General Kerr had dismissed Prime Minister Whitlam. In his reply, the Queen's secretary said that "it would not be proper" for the Queen "to intervene in person in matters which are so clearly placed within the jurisdiction of the Governor-General by the Constitution Act". In other words, these decisions were the Governor-General's responsibility. By the end of the 20th century, the only thing the Queen does for government in Australia is to appoint and dismiss the Governor-General and State Governors on the advice of the Prime Minister or relevant State Premier.

Does this mean that the Governor-General is the Head of State now? No; because the formal position described in the Constitution has not changed. Section 61 gives the Queen the "executive power of the Commonwealth" (even though it is "exercisable" by the Governor-General). Ministers are called the "Queen's Ministers" in section 64. The Governor-General is described as the Queen's representative in section 2 and again in section 68. The Queen remains Australia's constitutional Head of State even if the Governor-General does most of the work. This is a good example of how the way the Constitution works can change a lot in practice, even when the words stay the same.

What does the Head of State do?

The Constitution makes the Queen, represented by the Governor-General, part of both the Parliament and the executive government.

As far as the Parliament is concerned, the Queen's involvement is first explained in section 1. It says that the Parliament consists of "The Queen, a Senate and a House of Representatives". This does not mean that The Queen (or the Governor-General) actually sits in Parliament, of course (although the Governor-General opens each new main meeting or "session" of Parliament – usually, every three years). Their role comes at the end of the law-making process, when the Governor-General gives the Queen's "assent" to Bills which have been passed by the two Houses of Parliament.

Section 61 gives general executive power to the Queen and the Governor-General. The Governor-General also has other specific powers under the Constitution: to dissolve the House of Representatives, for example, or both Houses, if there is a deadlock. Most Acts of Parliament give other powers to the Governor-General as well.

But all of these powers are largely formal. In other words, they are written in the Constitution but in practice are not used by the Governor-General as he or she alone chooses. The Governor-General never refuses assent to a Bill, although people sometimes ask him to do so. And in making decisions under legislation, or under the Constitution itself, the Governor-General almost always acts on the advice of the government. The few exceptions to this are called the "reserve powers". They are described below.

There are hints in sections 62 and 63 that the Governor-General is expected to act on advice, but the Constitution does not say so very clearly. This part of our system of government depends largely on constitutional convention or things that have been done for a long time.

If you think about it, however, in most cases the Governor-General must accept the government's advice. The Governor-General might look very powerful in the Constitution. He has no control over Parliament at all, however. That means he has no access to money collected from taxes or "public money". Only a government with the confidence of the Parliament can persuade it to appropriate money, to enable the "executive power of the Commonwealth" to be used. The Head of State therefore depends on the executive government. And, in return, the executive takes responsibility for the decisions that are made.

Giving advice

The Constitution gives power to the Governor-General in two different ways.

Some sections mention only the Governor-General. Section 5, for example, says that the Governor-General can "appoint such times for holding sessions of the Parliament as he thinks fit". Section 57 says that the Governor-General can dissolve both Houses of the Parliament and call a joint sitting. Under section 64, the Governor-General appoints "officers to administer ... departments of State". In practice, these are the Ministers.

In most of these cases, the Governor-General acts on the advice of the Prime Minister. Sometimes the advice comes in the form of a letter and the letter is publicly released. The Prime Minister may also sign a decision by the Governor-General, to show that the government is taking responsibility for it.

Other sections of the Constitution give decisions to the "Governor-General in Council". The appointment of judges under section 72 is an example. All powers given by statute to the Governor-General are supposed to be exercised "in Council" as well. Section 63 of the Constitution explains that this means that the Governor-General is to act with the advice of the "Federal Executive Council". Under section 62, the Council consists of Executive Councillors "chosen and summoned" by the Governor-General who "hold office during his pleasure".

As usual, in this part of the Constitution, this does not mean quite what it says. As with almost everything else, in choosing and summoning an Executive Council the Governor-General acts on advice. Ministers must be Executive Councillors. Other people can be too: in particular, parliamentary secretaries and Ministers from previous governments. They will not be invited or "summoned" to an Executive Council meeting, however, unless the government wants them to be there.

The Executive Council, then, is the group which gives formal advice to the Governor-General. Normally, apart from the Governor-General, two or three Ministers or parliamentary secretaries will be there. They give the advice, which the Governor-General accepts. The final decisions are made in the Governor-General's name.

Why do we do it like this?

On the face of it, this seems an extremely complicated system. We give the Queen and the Governor-General all executive power but expect them to exercise it as the government says. Why do we do it this way? Surely it would be more efficient, and much easier to understand, if the government had executive power and was held directly responsible for its exercise and the Head of State was given whatever powers we actually want the Head of State to have.

Part of the explanation lies with history. At one time, the British Monarch had all executive power to use as he or she chose. As the Parliament became more powerful it refused to make laws or impose taxes or authorise spending unless the Monarch acted in a way which Parliament approved.

The idea that the Monarch should be advised by a government with the confidence of the Parliament developed naturally from there. Outwardly, everything remained the same. The Monarch kept the power. But the way in which it was used had really changed. And when the Australians drew up their own Constitution, they followed the same model. They gave formal power to the Head of State, but assumed it would be exercised on government advice.

The real question is whether this arrangement is still useful. In theory, it could be. An Executive Council meeting is the last stage before a final decision is made. It could be used by the government to have one last look at the decision. It could be used by the Governor-General to ask questions, before finally accepting the advice. In practice, however, an Executive Council meeting is largely a formality. It does not seem to add much to the quality of the decisions that a government makes.

Acting without advice

Sometimes, a Governor-General may make a decision without or even against advice. When this happens, he or she is said to be exercising "reserve" powers. The reserve powers are not written into the Constitution. They depend on constitutional conventions. To find out whether a reserve power exists we need to ask whether it has been exercised before and whether there is a good reason to have a reserve power of this kind.

There are three main areas in which the Governor-General can make a decision without advice in Australia.

1. The first concerns the appointment of the Prime Minister. One or other of the two main parties usually wins a clear majority of seats in the Parliament after an election. In this case, it is obvious who should be appointed Prime Minister. The "caretaker" Prime Minister advises the Governor-General to appoint this person, and the Governor-General acts on advice in the usual way.

    But it is easy to imagine times when a Governor-General might need to act independently. If no party won a clear majority, and a caretaker Prime Minister advised his own reappointment, the Governor-General would need to think carefully about it. And there is at least once instance in Australian history where the Governor-General exercised his own discretion. In 1975, having dismissed Mr Whitlam as Prime Minister, the Governor-General had no one to advise him about who to appoint next.

2. A "reserve" power may sometimes be used when the Prime Minister wants an early election. The Governor-General has constitutional power to dissolve the House of Representatives, which usually is exercised on advice. Even if the Prime Minister advises a very early

election, the Governor-General has to agree if the Prime Minister has the support of the House.

But if the Prime Minister has lost the support of the House and advises the Governor-General to call an election, the situation may be different. It may be best for the Governor-General to refuse the advice, if another Prime Minister can be found, who the House will support.

3. The third area is dismissal of the Prime Minister. We tend to think of this as controversial, because of the events of 1975, in which the Governor-General dismissed a Prime Minister who still had the confidence of the House, after the Senate refused to pass key money Bills. But the power can be useful in less controversial situations as well. If a Prime Minister who has lost the confidence of the House refuses to resign (which probably would never happen) we would expect the Governor-General to dismiss him or her, rather than letting the crisis continue.

In each of these three areas, the "reserve" powers help responsible government to work. The idea of reserve powers has developed together with responsible government and this is their main purpose. We have avoided the need to provide a complete constitutional framework for responsible government by leaving the Head of State with a choice on these key points.

It is sometimes suggested that there are other "reserve" powers, with the broader purpose of safeguarding the system of government as a whole. If that were correct it would, for example, justify the Governor-General's refusing assent to Bills which might be contrary to the Constitution or objectionable in other ways.

There are problems with this, however. A Governor-General is not necessarily the right person to make these kinds of decisions. And there are other ways of handling these problems. Unconstitutional Bills or even unlawful action by government can be dealt with by the courts. If there are particular aspects of the system of government which need better protection than they presently have it might be better to deal with this directly in the Constitution itself.

18

Who's who in Executive Government

A large pyramid

The executive branch of government is like a large pyramid. The Head of State is on top. Just below, come the Prime Minister and other Ministers. Further down come different people and groups or bodies: public service departments; commissions or boards or other authorities established by Act of Parliament; companies which government owns.

And there are other bodies, also, which you might be surprised to see. The Ombudsman, for example, or the Auditor-General (who reports to Parliament on government spending), or the Administrative Appeals Tribunal (which deals with appeals against some government decisions) or the Federal Police. We describe all these as part of the executive because they fit in better here than anywhere else.

Our system of responsible government means that Ministers at the top of the pyramid are responsible to Parliament for everyone below them. Exactly what this means, however, depends on the nature of the body itself. We expect Ministers to be more fully accountable for decisions taken in a department than for decisions of the Ombudsman or the Electoral Commission. Bodies like this are set up to be independent and Ministers have less control over them.

Ministers and Cabinet

The Prime Minister and the Ministers all are Members of Parliament. They are appointed by the Governor-General after an election. The Governor-General chooses the person with the confidence of the House of Representatives to be Prime Minister and the Prime Minister chooses the Ministers. They stay in government as long as they keep the support of the House of Representatives (and as long as the Senate agrees to pass the money Bills). The Prime Minister decides what responsibilities each Minister will have. These are known as his or her "portfolio". For example, the Minister for Health and Family services is responsible for public health, Medicare, health insurance, pharmaceutical benefits, and Aboriginal and Torres Strait Islander health services, among other things.

The Prime Minister also makes all or some of the Ministers members of "Cabinet". Cabinet is the main decision-making body in any government. It makes major new policies (for example, about nursing-home fees; or taxation reform; or who can own television and newspaper companies; or the number of people allowed to move to Australia). It decides what new laws Parliament will be asked to make. It makes the budget for the country, every year. Many Cabinet decisions must be approved by Parliament or by the Governor-General in Council before they take effect. This does not make Cabinet any less important, however. The Governor-General almost always does what Cabinet decides. Parliament usually does too.

Not all Ministers need be members of Cabinet. The Prime Minister may decide that it is more efficient to have a small Cabinet, with only the most important Ministers. When this happens, the other Ministers are said to be in the "outer Ministry". They still come to Cabinet meetings, however, when their portfolio is being discussed.

Ministers are responsible to Parliament individually and collectively or as a group. Individual responsibility means that Ministers must be responsible for decisions which they take and for what happens in their portfolio. If something goes wrong, they will not necessarily resign, but they will try to explain it and to fix it. Collective responsibility means that Ministers are jointly responsible for decisions which Cabinet takes. They have to stick together and defend a decision, for example, even if some of them think it was wrong. This is one reason why what happens in Cabinet meetings is confidential and why it is so hard to get information about them.

Offices of profit

There is an important constitutional rule that Members of Parliament cannot be paid by the government for doing any job other than their parliamentary one. You can find it in section 44 of the Australian

Constitution, which says that anyone who "holds any office of profit under the Crown" cannot be a Member of Parliament (or stand for Parliament). A long time ago, the purpose of this rule was to prevent the Monarch trying to win the support of Members of Parliament by giving them well-paid jobs. It is still useful, because it prevents the government from doing the same thing.

There is a possible problem with this rule in a system of responsible government, however. Responsible government requires Ministers to be Members of Parliament. Ministers are paid for their work and therefore have "offices of profit under the Crown". Section 44 recognises this and makes an exception for Ministers. If you look at the section you will see that it also makes a few other exceptions, which now are more difficult to explain.

Recently, governments have appointed some of their Members to a new position, called parliamentary secretary. Parliamentary secretaries are half-way between Ministers and ordinary backbench Members (Members who are not Ministers). They are supposed to help Ministers in various ways. They are even appointed as Executive Councillors, which means that they can advise the Governor-General at Executive Council meetings, if Ministers cannot go. Section 44 prevents them being paid extra salary, however.

Government departments

Each Minister is responsible for one or more departments. For example, the Treasurer is responsible for the Department of the Treasury and the Prime Minister is responsible for the Prime Minister's Department.

Historically, departments existed only to help Ministers. You can still find this relationship described in section 64. This section allows the Governor-General to "appoint officers to administer ... departments of State". If you read on, it becomes clear that those "officers" are also "the Queen's Ministers of State for the Commonwealth".

Nowadays departments still are there to help the government, but they also are important on their own. Some Acts of Parliament give decision-making powers directly to the Head of a Department (often called the "Secretary). Ministers and Secretaries may "delegate" or give the power to make many decisions to other officers in the Department. Decisions about visas and pensions, for example, often are made by quite junior officers in this way.

The relationship between Ministers and their Departments is a complicated one. In theory Ministers are responsible to Parliament for what goes on in their departments. They do not necessarily take the blame for mistakes made by the Department, however. The officer who made the mistake, or his or her boss, is likely to take the blame instead.

Ministers can direct their Departments to follow government policy and Departments must obey, as long as the policy follows the law. Our system also assumes, however, that Departments have some independence from their Ministers. Departments should provide expert advice, to help Ministers to make good policies. Departments should carry out policies which government make fairly. After an election is called, Departments should try to make sure that Ministers stick to routine jobs, consistent with their "caretaker" role.

Statutory bodies

Some activities of government are carried out by bodies set up by an Act of Parliament, instead of by Departments. These are called statutory bodies. This might be done to give the body greater independence, or to make it more professional or to make sure that it has an identity of its own separate from a Department or other governmental body. In these cases, the Act of Parliament gives decision-making powers directly to the people who are in charge of the statutory body. The National Crime Authority is an example. The National Gallery of Australia is another, very different one.

These Acts may also give power to a Minister. A Minister might be able to appoint people to particular positions, for example, or to give general directions in writing. The Minister cannot direct or control the body in any other ways, however. This is because decisions of Parliament override decisions of the executive government. If Parliament sets up a body to act in a particular way, that is how it must be.

Each of these bodies is part of some Minister's portfolio and Ministers must answer questions in Parliament about them. In practice, however,

Ministers cannot be expected to take the same amount of responsibility to Parliament for these bodies as for others over which they have more control.

Watchdogs

There are all sorts of watchdogs in our system of government. Some have been around for centuries. The Auditor-General is an example. The Auditor-General is a key link in Parliament's control of public money. He or she reports to Parliament on whether money has been spent for the purposes which Parliament approved and on other features of the spending which Parliament ought to know.

Some watchdogs are more recent. The Ombudsman deals with complaints about government decisions. This is an idea which Australia (and many other countries) have borrowed from Sweden. The Director of Public Prosecutions (DPP) decides whether to prosecute people suspected of having committed an offence. This used to be done by the Attorney-General, who is a Government Minister and therefore is elected to Parliament. The Director of Public Prosecutions was set up partly to keep these decisions separate from politics. The Privacy Commissioner keeps an eye on whether the information about private individuals which government collects is being used properly.

Watchdogs are only effective if they are independent of the executive government. But this is hard to guarantee, when the watchdogs themselves are appointed on the advice of Ministers and their budget is decided by the Cabinet each year. A lot depends on both the watchdogs and the Ministers understanding the roles they are supposed to play.

Government goes commercial

Recently, governments have begun to look more like private sector businesses. Governments themselves operate more commercially. More and more, governments are agreeing to contracts with companies or individuals to provide services which governments used to provide. Some parts of government are set up as companies, with government owning all the shares or only some of the shares.

These changes raise all sorts of questions for our current system of government. For example, how can government be responsible to Parliament for a company in which it doesn't own all the shares? How can Parliament make government accountable if information about a company or a contract is confidential and Parliament cannot see it? Should people be able to complain to the Ombudsman or to a tribunal about services provided using government money? Whatever answers we find to these questions need to be both workable and consistent with the principles of representative and responsible government.

19

Judges and courts

The Third Branch

We sometimes say that there are three "branches" of government. The first two are the Parliament and the Executive. The third is the courts. Members of courts usually are called judges or justices. Together, they make up the "judiciary". The whole system of courts is sometimes called the "Judicature". See the heading to Chapter 3 of the Constitution, for example.

Many people do not think of the courts as being part of government. That is a good thing, in a way, because courts are supposed to be independent of the other two branches. In fact, however, courts are absolutely necessary to the system of government. All communities need disputes to be settled peacefully, according to agreed rules which are applied the same way every time. This is the job of the courts.

What kinds of decisions go to courts?

Courts deal with argument or disputes which can be settled by law. There are many different kinds of disputes.

Sometimes disputes are between private individuals: over a car accident; or a will; or the boundary between two properties, for example.

Some disputes involve criminal charges. Examples include stealing; or manslaughter; or owning a gun without a permit.

Sometimes the government has to go to court because it seems that it has broken the law. This might happen, for example, if the government does not obey its own environment protection laws; or does not give someone a fair chance to explain before taking the pension away from them; or takes someone's property for a road, without providing "just terms" as the Constitution requires.

Who can go to court?

In practice, a dispute is only settled in court when someone takes it there. Whoever does this needs to have a special interest or be involved in the dispute in some way. The technical term is that they must have "standing". If you are supposed to receive a tax refund and you don't get it you can, if you want to, go to court. But you can't go to court to complain that your neighbour didn't get a refund even if you are very upset on his or her behalf. You would not have "standing".

If the dispute is over whether the government has broken the law and no single person is affected more than others, the question of standing is more difficult. Who should be able to take legal action (go to the court) to prevent illegal logging in a national forest, for example, or release of a blasphemous film? The decision at present is with the courts. They have been more generous in recent times in deciding who is allowed to bring disputes like this to court, but you still need to show a "special interest".

How do courts work?

Our approach to government uses the "adversary" system a lot. In other words, we assume that having two or more sides opposed to each other will bring out the best in both of them and produce the right result.

In the courts, the adversary system means that all parties (the people in the dispute) explain their case and a judge or group of judges decide the facts, apply the law and give judgment for one of the parties. In Australia judges must apply the Constitution, any relevant Commonwealth, State or Territory legislation and earlier decisions of any higher Australian court – which always includes decisions of the High Court. The judgment of each court in turn becomes binding on other courts below it.

Courts may look for guidance to other courts as well, elsewhere in Australia or overseas. Judgments of these other courts are not binding but they may be "persuasive", if the Australian court thinks that another court has found a good solution to a common legal problem. This is happening more and more, as modern technology makes the law of other countries easier to find.

Once a court makes its decision, if you don't think it was correct you may be able to appeal (go to) to a higher court for its decision. Otherwise, however, that will be the end of the matter.

Which court?

There are nine court systems or "hierarchies" in Australia: one for the Commonwealth and one for each State and Territory. Each State and Territory system begins with lower courts and goes up to a Supreme Court. The Commonwealth has a Family Court and a Federal Court and an Industrial Relations Court. At the top of all of them comes the High Court.

Which court you go to depends largely on the type of dispute. Minor disputes usually go to lower courts. More important disputes usually go to courts higher up the chain. Disputes over areas of State law (State jurisdiction) usually go to State courts. And these days, Commonwealth disputes (federal jurisdiction) go to federal courts more and more.

This does not have to happen, however. The Constitution gives the Commonwealth Parliament the choice whether to set up its own courts or to give "federal jurisdiction" to State courts. For the first 70 years after federation, the Commonwealth used State courts a lot. It now has its own courts as well, to deal with disputes under important Commonwealth Acts or with actions against the Commonwealth government. But some federal jurisdiction is still exercised by State courts particularly at the lower levels.

It is possible to have a dispute which involves both State and Commonwealth jurisdiction. It would be very inconvenient to have to go to two sets of courts for these. To deal with the problem, all Australian Parliaments have passed "Cross-Vesting" Acts. These make sure that every Australian court can deal completely with each dispute which comes before it. It is not clear whether cross-vesting is consistent with the Constitution. This is something for the High Court to decide.

The High Court

The High Court is Australia's highest court. Section 71 of the Constitution assumes that it will be established and this happened in 1903. Under the

Constitution, there must be a Chief Justice and at least two other Justices. At present there are six Justices of the High Court, in addition to the Chief Justice.

The High Court can hear appeals from any other federal court or any State Supreme Court. It plays an important role in ensuring that the common law is more or less the same, across all States. Because the High Court is the most important court, it deals only with the most important appeals. To get to the High Court, you need "special leave" (permission to have your case considered in the High Court) from the Court itself. The High Court will only grant special leave if there is a good reason to do so.

Some disputes can go to the High Court first. This is called "original jurisdiction". Section 75 of the Constitution gives the High Court some original jurisdiction, for example, where the Commonwealth itself is a party in a case. Section 76 lists some more, which the Commonwealth Parliament may give the Court. An important case that questions something in the Constitution may begin in the High Court, for example. If it is clear that the case is going to get to the High Court eventually, it will save a lot of time and money to start there first.

When the Constitution first took effect, in 1901, it was possible to appeal from the High Court to the Privy Council, in London. This can no longer happen and the High Court is Australia's court of final appeal.

Appeals to the Privy Council have been cut off in practice. If you read section 74 carefully, however, you will see that it is still possible to appeal to the Queen in Council (the Privy Council) on the "limits inter se" of the powers of the Commonwealth and the States if the High Court agrees to state or certify that the dispute ought to be dealt with by the Privy Council. Inter se questions are those which involve the boundaries of power between the Commonwealth and the States. The High Court gave a certificate once, in 1914, to allow the Privy Council to hear an appeal. It is very unlikely to do so again.

Being a judge

Think about the job which judges do and the circumstances in which they do it. Judges settle disputes between parties by applying the law. The law is often complicated. One party may be better educated, or more wealthy or more powerful than the others. It is important for both the parties and the communities to have confidence in the decisions which judges make.

To do this job properly, judges must be good at sorting out the facts of a dispute. They must be expert in finding which is the right law to use and applying it. And they must be independent, of the parties and of government. Judges must make the decision which they think is right in law. They must explain their reasoning in a way which the parties can understand. Their reasons must fit with the rest of the law and be able to be applied by other courts.

How can we ensure that judges have this mix of skills and independence?

The answer lies partly in appointing the right people in the first place. Under section 72 of the Constitution, judges are appointed by the Governor-General in Council. As we know from Chapter 17, this means the Governor-General acting with the advice of the Executive Council. In other words, Cabinet or a Minister (usually, the Attorney-General) really chooses the judges. The Constitution does not set out any qualifications for judges. It does not even require them to be lawyers. Most judges have been barristers, however, which means they have argued cases in courts before. They understand how courts work and they know a lot about the law themselves.

Appointments to the High Court are much the same, with one exception. Under the High Court of Australia Act, the Commonwealth is supposed to consult the States about appointments. This might mean anything, from allowing the States to suggest names to giving them a veto (the right to say no) over appointments. Currently, appointments to the High Court are made in a way that is somewhere in between these two extremes.

Under these arrangements, people with the right qualities can be appointed as judges, if governments use the appointment power well. The rest of section 72 is supposed to protect the independence of judges, after they are appointed. Judges keep their positions until they retire (aged 70, in the case of the High Court). Their salary ("remuneration") cannot be reduced while they are in office. They can be dismissed, but only through a public process which requires a good reason to be given. Both Houses of the Parliament must ask the Governor-General to dismiss a judge "on the ground of proved misbehaviour or incapacity". A judge who accepted a bribe, for example, or who was too ill to do the job any more, could be dismissed in this way.

Is this satisfactory?

Generally, the procedure for the selection of judges in Australia has worked well. Australia has had a long tradition of high quality courts and independent judges. But in recent years there have been questions about whether the appointment procedure should be more open. People have become more critical of judges, as of other institutions of government. They are more aware of the importance of the law-making role of courts. They are more suspicious of appointments which executive governments make. Questions are beginning to be asked about whether the courts should include more judges from different backgrounds.

The difficulty is to find another selection procedure which would work as well. Alternatives are to involve Parliament or a parliamentary committee; or to appoint a selection committee of judges and senior lawyers or of the community more widely; or to advertise for judges, to ensure that the government knows the field. The danger of all of these is that the best lawyers might not apply for the job and the quality of the courts might suffer. In the short term the answer is likely to be to require the executive government to consult more widely, perhaps explaining to Parliament what it has done but still leaving the final decision to be made by government alone.

20

Commonwealth or State

Different governments make different decisions

The earlier chapters have mainly talked about decisions by the Commonwealth Parliament or Commonwealth government or Commonwealth courts.

Not all decisions are Commonwealth decisions, however. Australia has other governments as well: six States; two mainland Territories; some external Territories, for example, Norfolk Island and the Cocos Islands; hundreds of local councils. Each of these governments is very important to the people who live in its area. To understand government decision-making properly, you need to know which government does what.

The division of power and responsibility between the Commonwealth and the States is particularly important. This is because they are the main partners in the federal system. They are established by the Constitution itself and get their authority from it. By contrast, the Territories are established and regulated by the Commonwealth government and Parliament and local government is established and regulated by the States. There are important questions, which were noted in Chapter 9, about how far the Commonwealth and the States should go in regulating or keeping an eye on other governments which are elected by their own communities (like ATSIC or local governments). There is no doubt that they can regulate them, however. And that is what makes the difference between one level of government and another.

The idea of a federal system

Chapter 3 described how and why Australia was established as a federal system. There were six separate colonies on the Australian mainland and in Tasmania. They wanted to form a single nation but to keep some independence as well. Representatives of the colonies drew up a

Constitution which created the Commonwealth as a national government and gave it appropriately national powers. But it also recognised the colonies, which now became States. It protected their existing Constitutions and laws and their remaining powers.

As our own history tells us, an important feature of a federal system is that it divides powers between different levels, or spheres, of government. Furthermore, it divides them in a special way, which gives each level of government some independence from the other. The States do not get their core powers from the Commonwealth and the Commonwealth does not get its powers from the States. The Constitution itself divides out powers between them. And within the limits of the system described below, neither can tell the other what to do.

The division of powers

We have already seen that there are three main kinds of government power: legislative, executive and judicial. All three are divided between the levels of government in a federal system. The Commonwealth has its own legislative, executive and judicial powers. And each of the States has its own as well.

The Constitution divides legislative power between the Commonwealth and the States in detail. The division of executive and judicial power is briefer, but describes the same general groups of powers. For example, the Commonwealth legislative power over "external affairs" is matched by an executive power to enter into treaties and jurisdiction over matters "arising under any treaty" in section 75(1). The division of legislative power therefore is a guide to the other two and is the main focus of the rest of this chapter.

There are many different ways of dividing power in a federal system. The Australian Constitution follows the United States model, which lists national powers and leaves all unlisted powers to the States. Forty Commonwealth powers or "heads of power" are listed in section 51. These powers are said to be "concurrent" which means that they can be exercised by State Parliaments as well.

A few Commonwealth powers are exclusive, which means that the States cannot exercise them at all. One of the most important is the power in section 90 to impose excise duties, which the High Court has interpreted to mean taxes on "goods" such as clothes, or food, or petrol, or cars. Another is the power over "Commonwealth places" in section 52 which includes, for example, airports and post-offices. Some other Commonwealth powers are effectively exclusive, because the Constitution takes State powers away. So, for example, States cannot have armed forces under section 114, or coin money under section 115.

Inconsistent laws

If the Commonwealth and the States can pass laws on the same matters, what happens when they are inconsistent or don't agree with each other? The answer is in section 109 of the Constitution. It says that the Commonwealth law will be the law that is followed, as long as it agrees with the Constitution. The inconsistent part of the State law will not operate at all.

An inconsistency is obvious, if the Commonwealth law says one thing, the State law says another and it is impossible to obey them both. But section 109 can be used in other circumstances as well. If a Commonwealth law deals with a subject completely (which is sometimes called "covering the field) a State law will not be able to interfere at all. So, for example, once the Commonwealth exercised its power over "marriage" in section 51(21) of the Constitution, there was no room for State Parliaments to make laws about marriage too, even if it would have been possible to obey them both.

Who has which powers?

The Commonwealth has all the powers listed in section 51. But why does it have these, and not others? Why should some powers be given to a national government in a federal system? Why should other powers be left to the States?

Section 51 itself provides some clues to the thinking of the framers of the Constitution. Some of the powers are obviously national: defence, naturalisation (becoming an Australian citizen), external affairs. Some have to do with how the government runs day to day, such as taxation, borrowing money and taking or acquiring property. Almost half the powers deal with aspects of trade and commerce (business), and show how important the framers thought creating a national market was. The Constitution mentions currency, banking, insurance, bills of exchange, bankruptcy and copyright to name a few.

Some powers cannot be exercised by a single State and so became the Commonwealth's. The interstate trade and commerce power is one of these. Only a few powers deal with social matters: marriage, divorce, some pensions and the "race" power over the "people of any race, for whom it is deemed necessary to make special laws". The last of these now enables the Commonwealth to make laws for the Aboriginal and Torres Strait Islander Peoples.

An important reason for giving power to the Commonwealth is to enable law to be the same throughout Australia. With two exceptions, however, the Constitution does not itself require uniformity of Commonwealth law. The first is that Commonwealth taxation must not "discriminate between States or parts of States". The second is listed in section 99 which says that the Commonwealth cannot give "preference" to any State or part of a State over another State or part of a State in "any law or regulation of trade, commerce or revenue".

There is a little flexibility in the division of powers between the Commonwealth and the States. As noted in Chapter 14, section 51(37) allows the Commonwealth to make laws on other matters, that the State Parliaments have asked it to or "referred" to it. The section has not been used much, because the States have not wanted to refer powers, but a few references have been made. Examples include air transport, meat inspection, parts of family law and the requirement for States to recognise each other's standards for goods and occupations, which is discussed in Chapter 26.

There is no separate list of State powers. As far as the Constitution is concerned, any power which is not a Commonwealth power is a State power. Some of the most important of these include criminal law, land management, education, health, transport and environmental protection.

Enforcement

The Constitution itself divides power between the Commonwealth and the States. Laws which are not consistent with the Constitution are invalid, or of no effect. Generally, both the Commonwealth and the States try to stay within their constitutional limits when making new laws. But sometimes it is hard to tell exactly what the limits are, particularly when circumstances have changed. Sometimes executive governments and Parliaments want to test the limits of their constitutional power.

If there is a dispute about the limits of power, eventually the courts must decide. If the dispute is serious enough, it will be decided by the High Court itself. Look again at the description of the powers in section 51 and you will see how difficult this task is. All of the powers are briefly stated: sometimes in only one or two words, such as "marriage" or "external affairs". Sometimes they are ambiguous or can mean more than one thing. For example, can a football club be a trading corporation, as mentioned in section 51(20)? And how can we tell whether a law is supported by a Commonwealth power or not? Is a law which gives tax relief to a company which trains its employees a law "with respect to" taxation? Is a law which prohibits a trading corporation from building a dam in Tasmania a law "with respect to" the corporation? Even when the Parliament really wants to stop the dam, and doesn't care at all who builds it?

Federal principles

The answer to all of those questions is yes. But you can see why the limits are uncertain. The words of the Constitution alone cannot always decide questions of this kind. The judges must be guided by underlying principles (the ideas and understanding that support the Constitution and our system of government). The Australian Constitution does not spell out these principles. The judges have had to develop them for themselves.

For the first 20 years after federation, the High Court interpreted Commonwealth powers in a limited way in order to preserve the scope of powers "reserved" to the States. If the power was ambiguous (which many of them are), the more limited interpretation was preferred.

This changed in 1920. In a very famous case called the *Engineers* case, the High Court said that Commonwealth powers should be read literally (what the words say), without making any assumptions about powers being reserved for the States. In the long term, this expanded the scope of Commonwealth power to the limits which the literal words describe.

The importance of this in practice can be seen by asking what are the limits to the power over "external affairs", in section 51(29). Obviously, this power lets the Commonwealth make laws about Australian diplomats (people who represent Australia officially in other countries) and representatives of other countries who are here. The High Court has said that it lets the Commonwealth make laws for things actually outside (external to) Australia (for example, mining in the Timor Sea). And the High Court has also said that the Commonwealth can use the power to make international treaties which Australia has signed part of Australian law. But treaties deal with a very wide range of subjects: postal services, air travel, human rights, the environment. It is difficult for the Court to say that only some of these are "external affairs" and not others. And so the Court has said that the power can be used to make any international treaty part of Australian law, even though some of these treaties deal with areas of State responsibility.

There is some remaining influence of federal principle, however. Federalism, at the very least, requires two levels of government. This means, the Court has said, that the Commonwealth cannot use its powers to discriminate against the States or between them. It certainly cannot use its powers to destroy the States or their ability to function. And within the limits of their power to legislate to affect the Commonwealth at all, the States cannot discriminate against the Commonwealth either.

Co-operation

The division of powers between the Commonwealth and the States is important, because it is the starting point for what each of them can do.

In real life, however, it is hard to put power into two boxes, one labelled Commonwealth and one labelled States. Some Commonwealth powers cut across State powers. The external affairs power, as we have seen, is an example. And many Commonwealth powers affect State powers in practice. A Commonwealth decision to increase the number of people immigrating to Australia, for example, means that the States need to provide more houses, and more places in schools.

In fact, there is a lot of co-operation between Australian governments. Ministers from different governments with similar responsibilities meet in

Ministerial Councils at least once a year and sometimes more often, to exchange information and to co-ordinate policies. The Commonwealth and the States co-operate in making law and administration uniform in areas ranging from the regulation of corporations, to the testing of food, to laws about adoption, to the control of financial institutions. Governments have entered into agreements to make environmental approval procedures more efficient. Co-operation of these kinds enables Australian governments to meet modern and changing needs. But it also means that what happens in practice can be different from what the Constitution says.

21

Money matters

Power and money

In a federal system, power to make decisions is divided between different levels or spheres of government. To make this work, we have to divide money between governments too. A government with responsibility for education needs to pay teachers to teach and build schools for them to teach in. A government with responsibility for transport needs money or capital to build roads or bridges or to buy buses or trains. Even if a government does not run schools or transport systems itself, it needs funds to ensure that services like this properly serve the whole community.

Governments get money from different sources. A lot of it is raised from people through taxes of various kinds. Some comes from charges for government services: water rates or car registration fees are examples. Some government money is borrowed and needs to be paid back, with interest (extra money), over a period of time. Some governments get money as grants from other governments, if they do not have enough of their own. In a federal system, the arrangements for setting up or raising taxes, borrowing money and sharing available funds can be as important to government decision-making as the power to make decisions itself.

What the Constitution says

With one important exception, the Constitution allows both the Commonwealth and the States to impose any taxes they like. The Commonwealth's tax power is in section 51(2) and simply refers to "taxation". The States can impose most taxes too, as far as the Constitution is concerned. And because the main purpose of taxing is to raise money for government, Commonwealth and State taxation laws can never disagree or "conflict" with each other, even if they tax the same thing. A State tax cannot be invalid under section 109 because it conflicts with a Commonwealth taxation law (although it might be invalid if it conflicts with another Commonwealth law).

The exception is in section 90 of the Constitution, which gives the Commonwealth "exclusive" power over duties of customs and excise. Duties of customs are taxes on goods coming into Australia or leaving it. The High Court has said that duties of excise are taxes on goods which are grown or made in Australia. In 1997, for example, the Court said that a very high licence fee imposed by New South Wales on people who sell tobacco was invalid. It was a tax on the tobacco and so it was an excise duty, which only the Commonwealth can impose.

The exclusive Commonwealth power over duties of customs and excise prevents the States imposing these important taxes. Why should this be, when the States can impose all other taxes, if they wish? As far as customs duties are concerned, the answer is clear. We want customs duties to be the same, in all parts of Australia. Someone who imports shoes into, say, New South Wales should pay the same tax as someone who imports them into Queensland. There is nothing to stop shoes going from New South Wales to Queensland (or vice versa) once they are in Australia.

The argument for exclusive Commonwealth power over excise duties is not as straightforward. Goods may be moved more easily throughout Australia if the taxes on them are the same. It is more convenient for people who make and sell goods to pay the same tax on them in every State. We may think that it unfair for Australians in one State to pay different taxes on goods than someone in a different State. But uniform sales taxes are not essential, even though they may be convenient.

The Constitution also limits the way in which both the Commonwealth and the States use their tax powers. Commonwealth taxation cannot discriminate or choose between States or parts of States, which really means that the taxes must be uniform. Neither Commonwealth nor State taxation can discriminate against inter-State trade so that it protects the trade of a particular State. The Commonwealth and the States cannot tax each other's property. This rule, which comes from section 114, also prevents local government from imposing rates on land owned by the Commonwealth.

The story of income tax

There is nothing in the Constitution to prevent the States imposing income tax. But, in fact, they don't. The reason is historical, and goes back to the Second World War.

When the war began, in 1939, all Australian governments imposed income tax. The Commonwealth wanted to take over income tax completely, in order to raise as much money as possible during the war. The Parliament passed four Acts which in practice prevented the States imposing income tax. The Acts imposed a very high Commonwealth tax, authorised taxpayers to pay the Commonwealth tax before any State tax, took over the system for collecting income tax in each State and gave to each State which did not impose an income tax, about the same amount of money it was giving up.

The States didn't think this was allowed by the Constitution and asked the High Court for its decision, but lost. Even those parts of the wartime tax system which would probably not be acceptable in normal times were supported by the defence power during the war. The Commonwealth has kept its control of income tax ever since.

In fact, however, most of the Acts which forced the States out of income tax are no longer in effect. Political reasons, rather than the Constitution, now prevent the States imposing income tax. The Commonwealth still raises a lot of money from income tax. A State income tax on top of that would be unpopular, at least if it resulted in higher taxes and two income tax forms. And the States became used to relying on the money from the Commonwealth government rather than imposing taxes, although that may be changing now.

Who taxes what?

In practice, therefore, the Commonwealth controls the two main sources of taxation: income tax and taxes on goods. Income tax has been the most important part of Commonwealth taxation, ever since the rates were increased during the war. The debate on a general sales tax, also known as a good and services tax or GST, is partly about broadening the kinds of Commonwealth tax and making the existing sales taxes simpler and more efficient.

The States impose other taxes: payroll tax, land tax, stamp duty, gambling taxes. Local government raises money from property rates, under State authority. These taxes are important, at least for the taxpayers. But the States cannot raise enough money for their own purposes from them. Only approximately 20 per cent of Australian taxation is raised by the States. By contrast, almost 50 per cent of all government spending is State spending, on areas of responsibility left to the States by the Constitution. This very large difference between the amounts the States can raise themselves and their spending needs is sometimes called the "vertical fiscal imbalance" or VFI. The difference is covered by money from the Commonwealth.

Redistributing revenue

From the time of federation, it was necessary for some money to be distributed from the Commonwealth to the States each year. At first, this was because the States had lost the power to impose customs duties, which was an important tax for all governments. More recently, the cause has been the wide definition of duties of excise, together with Commonwealth control of income tax. If excise duties mean all taxes on goods, as the High Court has said, then the States cannot impose taxes on goods at all.

The Constitution does not say much about how money should be distributed from the Commonwealth to the States. The framers themselves could not agree on the best arrangement and hoped that it would be worked out after federation. Chapter 4 of the Constitution describes in detail what should happen for the first few years. After that, section 94 simply required the Commonwealth to distribute its "surplus revenue" (extra money) to the States as it "deems (thinks) fair". As it has turned out, it was easy enough for the Commonwealth to manage its money in a way that does not leave a "surplus", even when things are going well. Because of this, section 94 has not been used at all.

Instead, money is distributed by the Commonwealth to the States under section 96, which allows the Commonwealth Parliament to grant "financial assistance" to a State "on such terms and conditions as the Parliament thinks fit". The amount which the States get is decided by the federal Cabinet each year. At present, the States are given about $15 billion each year, to use for their "general purposes". The rest of the money is "tied" in the way described below.

These arrangements have been criticised a great deal. We saw earlier how important money is for the workings of a parliamentary system. Governments need the support of their Parliaments, because only Parliaments can raise and appropriate funds.

Governments are responsible to Parliaments for the way in which their funds are spent. In Australia, the State governments spend a lot of money which has not been raised by their own Parliaments. And the Commonwealth Parliament raises a lot of money which is spent by the State governments.

One solution to this problem would be to change the tax system so that each Parliament raises enough money for its own needs. Another would be to accept that governments often depend on each other for funds in a federal system. This could be recognised by providing proper guidelines for distributing tax money in the Constitution itself.

Equal treatment

If the States receive about $15 billion each year in general funds, how is it distributed between them? The Australian States are very different from each other. Some can raise more money than others through their own taxes. Property is worth more in Sydney than in other parts of the country, for example. Some States have more young people than others, and so need more schools. Some States are bigger than others and need much longer roads.

Australia has developed a system of its own for distributing money between the States. It is called "fiscal equalisation".

Under this system, money or grants are distributed depending on the population of each State, adjusted to different State circumstances. These adjustments are calculated by an independent organisation (another watchdog): the Commonwealth Grants Commission. Usually, the Commonwealth and the States accept these calculations. The Commission considers the ability of each State to raise its own money and the amount each State needs to spend to provide government services like those in other States. Whether States use the grants to provide similar services, however, is up to them to decide.

Tied grants

Approximately another $15 billion goes from the Commonwealth to the States each year for particular purposes, on conditions set by the Commonwealth Parliament under section 96. These are called "tied grants". Some of the most important of these are health, hospitals, education, transport and some social service programs.

These grants increase the money available to the States for areas of State responsibility. Another important result of this is that they also allow the Commonwealth to influence the way in which the money is spent. The High Court has said that there are no limits on the conditions which say how the grants must be spent. Using tied grants, the Commonwealth Parliament can set literacy standards for schools, or change procedures for service delivery in hospitals or require a report looking at the effect a development project could have on the environment before the development begins. The conditions which the Commonwealth puts on grants can be as detailed as it wants them to be.

Using tied grants effectively changes the way powers are distributed by the Constitution. States do not have to accept a grant, but usually they do. Through grants, the Commonwealth can implement its policies on many different things for which it has no constitutional responsibility at all.

Borrowing

All governments borrow money to pay for capital projects that will benefit Australians in the future as well as Australians now: schools, hospitals, railway systems, freeways. Obviously, we want this money to be borrowed on the best terms available. And we do not want governments to borrow more than they need.

In Australia, borrowing by all governments is co-ordinated through an organisation called the "Loan Council". The Commonwealth and all State and Territory governments all have representatives on this Council. The Loan Council is set up by an agreement between governments called "The Financial Agreement". The Financial Agreement is unique as compared to all other agreements, because it has a base in the Constitution in section 105A. This section 105A was included in the Constitution in 1928, when the first Financial Agreement was signed. It authorises the Commonwealth to make agreements with the States which deal with their "public debts". Surprisingly perhaps, it also says that agreements can override anything else in the Constitution itself.

Earlier versions of the Financial Agreement required the Commonwealth to borrow money for all governments. The present agreement requires governments to tell the Loan Council how much they want to borrow, but then allows each government to borrow for itself. The idea here is that the financial markets and other kinds of political pressure will keep government borrowing within reasonable limits, as long as information about the borrowing is publicly available. And, so far at least, this appears to be right.

22
Rule of law

Governing within limits

All democratic governments are limited in what they can do and how they can do it. Some important limits may be laid down in a Constitution. Other limits may be found in Acts of Parliament or in the common law or in practices which have been followed for a long time.

Limits on how things are done are very common. Their purpose may be to make sure that government does not become too powerful or that decision-makers are accountable or that decisions are fair. These "procedural" limits may, for example, separate powers between branches of government. Different parts of government may be designed to check and balance each other. Governments may need to pay money to make up for something that has happened (when they take someone's property, for example) or make laws publicly available or give reasons for decisions which they make.

Some of the most important limits are connected with democracy. Governments and Parliaments cannot go on without an election for longer than a fixed period which usually is three or four years. But "substantive" limits may be placed on government for other reasons as well. The community may agree on certain basic standards or values which it wants preserved, no matter what. However strong our belief in democracy, we may accept that there are certain things which the majority should not be able to do, or ways in which the interests of individuals or minority groups should be respected. Allowing everyone to practise their own religion is an example. Even some of our economic goals may require government action to be limited. In Australia, for example, no government can stop people from moving between the States.

Different countries have different ideas about what the limits on government should be, how they should be imposed and how they can be justified. All of them are trying to strike a balance between effective government on the one hand and a fair and peaceful society on the other.

All are influenced by the history and circumstances of their own communities. The next few chapters consider the limits on government in Australia.

Rule of law

Whatever other limits are placed on government, all democratic societies observe a collection of principles known as the rule of law. The rule of law affects us all. Importantly, it affects governments too.

The rule of law means that everyone, including government, has to obey or be subject to the law. It means that people know what the law is, or at least, can find out. It means that law is applied by courts, which are independent from outside influence, including government.

Some people argue that the rule of law means more than this. They say that the rule of law requires the laws themselves to meet basic standards. In other words, it is not much use requiring everyone to obey the law, if the law itself is bad. On this view the rule of law would, for example, prevent laws from discriminating against people and require them to respect basic rights to life and liberty.

The rest of this chapter explains the meaning of the rule of law in Australia and how much the Constitution protects it.

Everyone is subject to law

In Australia, we believe that no one should be above the law. The Constitution applies to everyone. Acts of Parliament and the common law also apply to everyone, unless there is a good reason why they shouldn't. The courts deal with all legal disputes, no matter who the people or organisations in the dispute may be.

Historically, there were exceptions for government in some circumstances. Governments could not be taken to court by someone who thought that it had broken a contract or had caused injury to someone (committed a tort). It was understood that Acts of Parliament didn't apply to governments unless it was really necessary. These "immunities" of government from law have almost disappeared. Legislation has made it possible for governments to be taken to court for problems with contracts and for torts.

And while the High Court still begins with an assumption that an Act of Parliament does not apply to government, it is more easily persuaded that it does.

The High Court has also limited the immunity which Commonwealth and State governments have from each others laws. This immunity has not completely gone, however. For example, section 114 of the Constitution prevents the Commonwealth and the States from taxing each other's property. And sometime, governments are able to claim "privilege" so that they don't have to give certain information in court, because it would not be in the public interest to release it.

The idea that in principle everyone is subject to law does not necessarily mean that everyone is subject to the same law. The question whether laws should deal with people equally or without discrimination is discussed in the last part below. It is a fact of life, also, that some people can defend themselves in court better than other people, because they have more money and can afford a good lawyer, or because they can explain themselves and their actions more clearly. It may never be possible to correct these inequalities completely but we need to be aware that they exist.

The law is known and certain

People need to know the laws which apply to them, in order to obey them. For the same reason, people need to understand what laws mean. Laws should not be "retrospective", or backdated so as to change the law which applied when the reason for the legal dispute took place.

Australian law follows these guidelines pretty well. All Acts of Parliament are published. So are the most important decisions of courts. We accept that, in principle, new laws should only begin to work from the time they are made. There is no constitutional requirement for any of this, however. And there are some exceptions. Legislation to impose new taxes often takes effect from the date when the taxes are announced by the executive government, rather than from the time the Parliament passes the law. Other legislation may be retrospective as well. For example, in 1988, the Commonwealth Parliament passed a law to make it illegal in Australia to commit "war crimes" (for example, murder with the intention of destroying an ethnic group) in Europe during the Second World War. The High Court said that the law was valid, even though it was retrospective.

The idea that the law is known and certain is affected in other practical ways as well. Many Acts of Parliament and decisions of courts are hard to understand, even when you read them. Laws made by government under authority delegated by Parliament are not published as regularly as they could be. Court decisions sometimes change the meaning of law with retrospective effect. International treaties which must be followed by Australia (although not by individual Australians) and are not regularly published either. There are many ways in which we can improve the way we do things. But acceptance of the basic principles is important nevertheless.

Independent courts

The rule of law requires law to be explained or interpreted and enforced by independent courts which are expert and fair.

The ways in which Australia protects the independence of judges and courts were considered in Chapter 19. Judges are appointed by the Governor-General or State Governor (on the advice of the executive government), to show the importance of their position. Because judges are appointed until they retire and their salaries are protected, they don't have to worry about losing their job and so they aren't influenced by what the government wants to do. These rules are important, but not sufficient to make sure judges are independent. Judicial independence relies very heavily on self-restraint by governments and parliaments. In return, courts are expected to confine themselves to making judicial decisions and to keep out of public debate.

Judicial independence generally is respected in Australia. But in recent years, there have been some pressures on it. Court decisions on issues about which some people feel strongly (for example, native title and free speech) have caused criticisms of the courts, as well as of the decisions themselves. One criticism, made by some elected representatives, is that courts have gone beyond their judicial role and begun doing what only elected representatives should do. Many people would not agree with this criticism, although others do. The fact that there is disagreement shows how delicate the balance is between what courts do and what the other branches do. Whoever is right, however, conflict between the courts and the other branches of government could hurt judicial independence. Executive governments might be tempted to appoint judges who are more likely to agree with them. Judges may be influenced by the controversy over particular issues to come to different decisions. The conflict could affect community confidence in the courts, on which the rule of law depends.

The courts can only play a role in applying the law if they have the power or "jurisdiction" to do so. The idea of the rule of law means that some courts somewhere should have jurisdiction if a legal dispute arises. The jurisdiction of courts usually can be taken away by Parliament, however. Parliament might want to do this where an Act of Parliament gives executive government authority to make sensitive decisions (for example, about migration) and the government does not want the courts to get involved. Sections of Acts which remove the jurisdictions of courts are called "ouster" clauses.

The jurisdiction of the High Court is more secure. Section 75(5) of the Constitution itself gives the High Court jurisdiction in cases involving the Commonwealth or government officers. The Commonwealth Parliament cannot prevent the High Court from dealing with cases of this kind.

The content of law

We in Australia tend to think of the rule of law as being procedural rather than substantive. In other words, we agree that the law must be known and applied to everyone through independent courts, but we do not worry so much about setting standards which the laws themselves should meet.

This is largely because, for most Australians at most times, the law has in fact been reasonable and fair. Generally, Parliaments make laws which try to treat people equally and which respect basic individual rights. There is nothing in the Constitution which requires this to happen, however. One question for the future is whether we will continue to rely on governments which are supported by the majority in Parliament to treat all Australians fairly, or whether the Constitution should say more about how this should happen than it does now.

23

Checks and balances

What do checks and balances do?

Governments are limited in the way they do things by checks and balances on power. Decisions made by one part of government may be stopped (or checked) by another. For example, the High Court may find that Acts of Parliament don't agree with the Constitution. At the same time, however, the executive government makes appointments to the High Court and Parliament provides money for it. In this way, the powers of these parts of government are "balanced".

One purpose of checks and balances is to prevent any part of government becoming too powerful. This may help to protect the rights and liberties of people. Checks and balances also help to make sure that decisions are made properly and publicly and that there is accountability for them.

The parliamentary system which we use in Australia tends to concentrate power. The rule that the government is chosen because it has the confidence of the House of Representatives means that the House of Representatives usually does what the executive government wants. If Parliament was made up of just the House of Representatives, this combination would be very powerful indeed because Parliament has supreme power, within the guidelines found in the Constitution.

Parliament does not consist of the House of Representatives alone, however. It also includes the Senate, which is a check on the House of Representatives. And there are other checks and balances in the system as well. Like the Senate, some of these are in the Constitution. They are enforced through the courts and cannot be changed without a referendum. One of the most important is the separation of powers between the executive, the legislature and the judiciary, which is discussed in the next chapter. The federal system is another kind of constitutional check and balance. So, in some circumstances, is the Governor-General. The power of the executive government, supported by the House of Representatives, in turn, checks other institutions as well.

Some checks and balances are not protected by the Constitution. These include an independent public service to carry out government policy fairly; an Auditor-General, to ensure that public funds are properly spent; an Electoral Commission to supervise the fairness of elections; an Ombudsman to deal with complaints about government. These organisations could be made less effective as a check and balance because their responsibilities can be changed by Parliament. But they are important in the Australian system of government, all the same.

The Senate

The Senate and the House of Representatives are checks on each other because laws made by the Commonwealth Parliament have to be approved by both Houses. As the House of Representatives potentially is the more powerful House, the role of the Senate as a check on the power of the House is more important.

As we saw in Chapter 12, the Senate and the House of Representatives are likely to have different views on some proposed laws. This is partly because they are elected under different election systems and, in the case of half the Senate, elected at different times. The result tends to be that independent and small parties are represented in the Senate and neither the government nor the opposition has a majority there.

In addition to the differences caused by the electoral systems, some voters deliberately vote for different parties in the two Houses, to encourage one to act as a check on the other. And, sometimes, the differences exist because the two Houses look for different things. The majority in the House of Representatives is likely to support government policy, whatever it may be. The Senate is more free to begin by considering whether a Bill is fair and respects people's rights. In the end, however, Senators will follow their party policy too, if there is a conflict with other standards.

As with all checks and balances, we sometimes worry about whether the Senate offers too much of a check and whether the balance of power between the House and the Senate is right. Checks and balances are important, but we want government to be effective and to represent the view of a majority of voters, as long as this view is a reasonable one.

This is the main reason why the Senate does not provide a total check on the wishes of a government in the House of Representatives. As described in Chapter 12, if there is a deadlock between the Senate and the House of Representatives, both Houses may be dissolved to give voters a say. If the deadlock continues after the election, a joint sitting of both Houses may be held to vote on the Bill or Bills on which the two Houses cannot agree. A Bill will become law if it is passed at a joint sitting by a majority of all Members of the House of Representatives and Senators. As the government usually (but not always) has a clear majority in the House of Representatives and usually is just short of a majority in the Senate, the views of the House of Representatives and the government are likely to win in a joint sitting. This was the result of the only joint sitting held so far, in 1974.

The federal system

The federal system is a check and balance because it divides power between governments. No government in Australia can do everything. Acting together, Australian governments can do almost everything, but they don't usually act in that way. More often than not, the various governments represent different political parties. On the unusual occasions when the same party is in government everywhere, the governments still do not work as closely together as you might think they would.

There are some obvious examples in Australian history where the federal division of powers has acted as a check on one level of government in a way which has prevented what many would consider a misuse of power.

In 1951, for example, the High Court said that the Commonwealth Parliament did not have enough power of its own to get rid of the Communist Party. In 1982, a Commonwealth Act using the external affairs power in section 51(29) of the Constitution prevented the Queensland government discriminating against some Aboriginal Australians who wanted to buy a lease of a pastoral property. In 1994, Tasmanian legislation which discriminated against gay men was overruled by a law of the Commonwealth Parliament. This law had been passed after a decision of the Human Rights Committee of the United Nations said that the Tasmanian Act was against international law.

The federal system does not necessarily prevent power being used badly, of course. Under our system, what Parliaments do generally is up to them and to the voters who elect them. The federal system means, however, that even if one government and Parliament does not work particularly well, that will not affect all decisions that are made. The Commonwealth government and Parliament can made decisions only on particular subjects. And State governments and Parliaments can make decisions only for their own State.

The Head of State

It is sometimes said that the Queen and the Governor-General are a check and balance in the Australian system of government as well. If this is right, it needs to be considered in designing a system to replace the Queen, if Australia decides to become a republic instead of a constitutional monarchy.

The main argument for the Head of State as a check and balance is the discretionary or "reserve" powers which may be used by the Governor-General if there is a hitch in the working of responsible government. As we saw in Chapter 17, the Governor-General can decide who to appoint as Prime Minister after an election if no party or coalition of parties has a majority in the House. He can refuse to give an early dissolution of the House of Representatives to a Prime Minister who has lost control of the House if someone else might have it. He can fire a Prime Minister who has lost the support of the House or can't get the Senate to agree to key money Bills and refuses to resign or call an election. In each of these cases, the Governor-General has a role because there is no Prime Minister with the necessary level of support from Parliament. The Governor-General therefore acts as a check on the Prime Minister in rare but important situations.

It is sometimes said that the Head of State acts as a check and balance in the system in other situations as well. For example, many government decisions are made by the Governor-General in the Federal Executive Council. Depending on how the Executive Council works, this might be a chance for decisions to be looked at again. The Constitution also gives the Governor-General other powers (for example, to approve or give "assent" to Bills) which you might think he could use in whatever way he thinks is right. And it is sometimes said that the Queen has a check and balance role as well. Perhaps she can refuse to appoint someone as Governor-General, if they wouldn't be good for the job. Perhaps she can stop a Prime Minister getting rid of a Governor-General who is doing well, but who the Prime Minister does not like.

It might be comforting to think that the Queen and the Governor-General can act in these ways, but in fact they don't, as far as we know.

The Executive Council in fact is just a formal meeting in which advice is given and taken. Of course it is possible that the need to put a decision through another process could cause it to be changed but, in practice, that does not happen. By the time a decision gets to the Executive Council, a Minister or the Cabinet have already made up their minds. Some decisions even are announced by the government before the Executive Council meets.

There is no ground for believing that a Governor-General will use extra reserve powers, either. The monarch in Britain has not refused assent to a Bill since the early 1700s and the Governor-General has never refused assent. Nor, with one exception, are there examples of other reserve powers being used. The exception is that in 1932 Governor Game of New South Wales sacked Premier Jack Lang because he was breaking the law. Some people think that this means that there is one other reserve power in Australia, to sack a Prime Minister who is acting unlawfully. Other people think that these are questions which are better left to the courts.

If extra checks and balances are needed, beyond the reserve powers which are needed to make responsible government work, the Governor-General may not be the best person to provide them. Under our present arrangements, the Governor-General is appointed by the Queen on the advice of the Prime Minister. He cannot reasonably be expected to be a check on the power of the Prime Minister who advised his appointment. And anyway, a Governor-General cannot act against the wishes of a government with the support of the House of Representatives, at least unless he can get another government with the support of the House quickly. One problem of believing that the Governor-General might be more of a check and balance than it is possible for him to be is that it prevents us considering other types of checks and balances which will really work. If we are worried about the kind of legislation which Parliament might pass, for example, it would be better to put more guidelines in the Constitution about what Parliament is able to do.

Nor can we expect the Queen to act as a check on the Prime Minister in appointing or removing a Governor-General. The reigning King or Queen has accepted Australian advice about the Governor-General since 1929. It may be that the need for the Queen to appoint the Governor-General has some effect on the choice which the Prime Minister makes, but this is only guessing. Similarly, in principle, the Queen would have to accept a Prime Minister's advice to remove a Governor-General before his term finished, although this has never been done. The Queen may delay accepting the advice in these circumstances, but in the end she would have no choice.

24

The separation of powers

The idea of separation of powers

Most western constitutional systems agree that there are three main kinds of government power: legislative power; executive power and judicial power. Most also agree that the powers should be used by three different branches: a legislature (or Parliament); an executive; and a judiciary. The reason for this is partly because it is good for different powers to be exercised in different ways, as discussed in Chapter 15. Most importantly, however, the separation of powers is a way of limiting power. If power is divided between different branches of government, no single branch can be too strong.

Separation of powers supposes that you can tell which powers are legislative, which are executive and which are judicial, although that is not always easy in practice. What sort of power does the Industrial Relations Commission use, for example, when it sets new working conditions through an award, to settle an industrial dispute? Different countries also have different ideas about how separate the three branches of government should be. None of the branches can be completely separate from each other, because all are part of the same system of government.

What the Constitution says

The systems of government in the Commonwealth and all Australian States and Territories draw distinctions between legislative, executive and judicial power and expect them to be used by different branches of government, at least as a starting point.

The Commonwealth is different from the other governments in Australia, however, because its separation of powers is required by the Constitution itself. This means that if any branch of the Commonwealth government uses the wrong power, whatever it has done can be declared illegal by a court.

The Australian Constitution does not actually say that there is a separation of powers. The High Court (and, long ago, the Privy Council) has accepted that there is, however. The main reason given for this finding is the form of the Constitution. We have already seen how the first three chapters deal separately with the Parliament or legislature, the executive government and the judicature or courts. Each chapter begins with a statement about where the power for that branch of government is located. So Chapter 1 begins with section 1, which says that "The legislative power of the Commonwealth shall be vested in a Federal Parliament ...". Chapter 2 begins with the statement in section 61 that "The executive power of the Commonwealth is vested in the Queen ...". And, similarly, Chapter 3 begins with section 71, which opens by saying that "The judicial power of the Commonwealth shall be vested in a Federal Supreme Court, to be called the High Court of Australia ...".

The constitutional separation of powers has not been very important for legislative and executive power (although even here it has some effect). By contrast, it has made a big difference to the way in which judicial power is used, as we will see below.

Legislative and executive power

The separation of legislative and executive power is complicated in a parliamentary system like ours.

The first complication is that Ministers, who are at the centre of executive government are also Members of Parliament. Ministers come from the political party or coalition which the House of Representatives is prepared to support. They stay on as Members of Parliament after they have been appointed as Ministers. They remain in government as long as they have the support of the Parliament. And, in practice, the government controls the House of Representatives. The legislature and the executive are still separate bodies in our system, but they are very closely linked.

Not only are the executive and the Parliament linked in these ways, but executive and legislative power overlap as well. Parliament can override executive power, if it wishes to do so. Signing treaties, for example, is an executive power, but Parliament could get rid of it tomorrow by passing an Act which said that, in the future, all treaties must be approved by Parliament itself. And at the same time, Parliament gives a lot of its power to the executive government, to make minor laws. When this happens, the executive uses legislative power too.

Even though it has said that there is a three-way separation of powers, the High Court has allowed all this overlapping of power to continue. And, indeed, it hardly has a choice. The Constitution itself requires Ministers to be Members of Parliament. The rule that Parliament can override executive power is part of the common law, on which our Constitution was built. Legislative power has been given to the executive for a long time in all parliamentary systems. It saves Parliament's time. And it is acceptable enough in principle, as long as the power given to the executive is not too important and Parliament supervises the way in which it is used.

Some other countries have a very different kind of separation of powers. The United States is one example of this. In the United States, the President (or executive) and Congress (or the legislature) are elected, separately from each other. The President holds the job for four years and does not depend on the support of either House of Congress. The President has executive power under the Constitution. Legislative power is given to Congress. The powers are equal. Neither can be given to another branch of government. Neither can override the other. Checks and balances apply between the branches themselves, however. The President can stop Acts of Congress, unless a very large number of Members of Congress are in favour of them. The Congress can "impeach" or remove the President, in circumstances set out in the Constitution.

Separation of judicial power

The courts are quite separate from the other branches of government, and it is possible for judicial power to be separate too. In fact, under the Australian Constitution it is very separate indeed. The High Court has said that only the three kinds of courts set out in section 71 of the Constitution can use federal judicial power. They are the High Court, other federal courts set up by the Commonwealth Parliament and "other" courts, which in fact are State courts. Federal courts, which include the High Court, cannot use anything but judicial power.

Again, there is nothing in the Constitution which clearly says that this is what separation of judicial power means. In agreeing to these principles, the High Court pointed to the way in which Chapter 3 of the Constitution specifies which courts can do what. These principles can be defended also as a way of protecting judicial independence from the other two branches of government.

A rule which says that only courts can use federal judicial power makes it necessary to be able to identify a court and to define judicial power.

A federal court is one which meets the requirements of section 72 of the Constitution. Most importantly, the members of a court (the judges) must be appointed by the Governor-General until they retire. A body which is called a court and has members who are called judges will not be a federal court unless it is set up in this way. As we have seen, federal judicial power can be exercised by State courts as well. These courts are set up under State Constitutions or other State laws. They don't have to satisfy section 72 although the High Court has said that they must not work in a way which does not agree with the use of federal judicial power.

Judicial power is the power to give a decision about rights and duties, based on existing law, which must be followed. The definition is hard to apply in border-line cases. In 1995, for example, in *Brandy's* case the High Court was asked to decide whether the Human Rights and Equal Opportunity Commission (HREOC) was using judicial power even though it was not a court. Under a law made by the Parliament, HREOC was given power to deal with complaints that one person had discriminated against another, because of their race. The findings which HREOC made in each case were sent to the Federal Court and automatically took effect, unless the person about whom the findings were made asked for a review by the court. The High Court said that HREOC was using judicial power and that this went against the separation of judicial power under the Constitution.

The kinds of cases which can be heard by federal courts are set out in sections 75 and 76 of the Constitution. Both sections use the word "matter" to describe these decisions. This simple word has turned out to be very important as well. The High Court has said that federal jurisdiction must involve a real issue of some kind.

One effect of this has been to stop the High Court from answering questions from government about whether a Bill before Parliament agrees with the Constitution. Courts which do this (for example, the Supreme Court of Canada) give "advisory opinions". Advisory opinions are a way of settling arguments about whether a Bill which Parliament is considering agrees with the Constitution or not. But sometimes it is difficult for a court to make a decision of this kind, unless there is a real dispute. Asking a court to give an opinion before a Bill is passed also makes the court look like an adviser to the Parliament or to the executive government. It might make the courts seem less independent than they ought to be.

Why the separation of judicial power matters

Separation of judicial power under the Constitution makes an important difference to the way Australian government works.

In the first place, it has prevented courts from being given powers which are not judicial. Federal courts could not be asked to negotiate or arbitrate industrial disputes, for example, because arbitration is an executive (or perhaps legislative) power. Federal courts could not be asked to agree to continue keeping dangerous offenders in gaol after they have served their sentence, as some State courts have been. That power is not judicial either.

Separation of judicial power has also prevented other bodies using judicial power. Over the years, this has had its main effect on organisations which are set up to deal with disputes of various kinds but which do not meet the definition of a court. One of the first of these was the "Interstate Commission", set up under section 101 of the Constitution itself. The Interstate Commission was supposed to have powers of "adjudication and administration" over disputes about how the sections of the Constitution dealing with economic matters worked. In 1915, the High Court said that whatever those words meant, the Commission could not use judicial power because its members were appointed only for seven years and so it was not a court. This made the Commission much less important. It now no longer exists at all.

Other tribunals have run into the separation of judicial power as well. For example, the Trade Practices Commission (now the Australian Competition and Consumer Commission) had to be carefully set up, so as not to disagree with separation of powers. HREOC had to be changed, when the High Court said that it was using judicial power. The Native Title Tribunal may have been in trouble for the same reasons.

Separation of judicial power means that Parliament cannot use judicial power either. This is important for the protection of individuals under the Constitution. For example, Parliament cannot pass a law to say that a particular person has committed a crime and to punish them for it, because this is judicial power. Separation of judicial power may also limit the instructions which Parliament can give the courts about how to do their work.

Exceptions

Like many constitutional rules, there are exceptions to this one.

Some are specific and limited. Rule-making is a legislative power, but courts need to make some rules about how the courts are supposed to work, which are called Rules of Court. The defence forces use courts called "Courts Martial" to deal with cases when someone in the forces breaks their rules, even though this is judicial power and courts martial they are not set up in a way which agrees with Chapter 3 of the Constitution. Either House of Parliament may decide whether someone has acted in a way which prevents Parliament performing it functions and so is in "contempt of Parliament". In some circumstances, refusing to give information to a parliamentary committee might be contempt of Parliament, for example. In theory, Parliament can put these people in gaol, although that would be a politically difficult thing to do.

There is one other, more general exception, as well. The High Court has agreed that although courts can only use judicial power, people who are judges may be appointed to other organisations (like tribunals) or may be given power which is not judicial, as individuals. The argument for doing this is that people who have the qualities which make them good judges (such as a reputation for independence and the ability to work out complicated facts) may be very useful for other purposes as well.

This way of getting around the separation of judicial power has been used a lot. It allows judges to be appointed to the Administrative Appeals Tribunal, for example. It even allows judges to give permission for the police to tap telephone calls. The exception seems to have reached its limit, however. The High Court has now said that judges cannot be asked to do things which are incompatible, or don't agree with their judicial function. For example, a judge cannot be asked to make a report to a Minister about whether Aboriginal heritage is being threatened, before the Minister uses a power to stop it. And in another recent development, the High Court has said that State Parliaments cannot require State courts to do anything "incompatible" with their judicial function either, because State courts also use federal judicial power under the Constitution.

25

Protecting rights

Constitutions and rights

The constitutions of some countries limit what government can do, in ways which protect the rights of people. Limits of this kind have different effects, depending on what they are intended to achieve.

Sometimes they guarantee that people will be able to do certain things, no matter what government decides. Free speech, or the right to protest, or the right to join any kind of association, for example, often are protected in these ways. Some limits prevent government from doing certain things to people. They may prevent someone's house being searched, without proper authority, for example, or prevent discrimination against them on grounds of race, or sex or religion.

And sometimes constitutions limit the way in which government deals with people. People may be arrested, for example, if they are suspected of having committed a crime. But they must be told why they have been arrested. And they must be brought before a court quickly and given a fair trial.

Some of the most recent constitutions also say that the government must use its power in ways which most probably achieve particular results: a healthy environment, for example, or decent housing or basic health care.

Most constitutions put limits of these kinds together and call them a "Bill of Rights", or sometimes a "Charter of Rights". If the limits are part of the original constitution, usually they come towards the beginning because they are recognised to be so important. The Constitutions of South Africa and Germany are examples of this. Where the limits are set by changes to the constitution after it is passed, they may come in a separate document, or at the end of the Constitution, as in Canada and the United States. In all of these cases, however, the Bill or Charter of Rights is part of the constitution. This means that it can be changed only in the same way as the rest of the constitution, unless the constitution itself says something different.

Individual rights or interests which a constitution protects in this way are those considered most important by that particular society. So, for example, the Canadian Charter of Rights and Freedoms protects the rights of Canadians to speak either English or French, and the rights of the Aboriginal peoples, because these were the original communities in Canada. But there is a common core of basic rights which appear in most constitutions: to life, liberty and personal safety; to freedom of religion and belief; to freedom of expression, assembly and association; to vote and to stand for election; to equality before and under the law; to fair treatment by the police and by courts; to own property. Many of these rights also are recognised by the common law. And most of them are included in international agreements to which many countries (including Australia), belong.

The Australian Constitution and rights

The Australian Constitution does not have a Bill of Rights, for the reasons explained in Chapter 13. The British parliamentary tradition, on which much of our system of government is based, did not give rights constitutional protection. In the case of Britain itself, constitutional protection of rights was impossible because there was no single, written Constitution which was more important than ordinary laws. The British Parliament was "sovereign" in the sense that it had total power. It was believed that Parliament would not use this power badly, especially as a wider range of people were given the right to vote. And it was believed also that independent courts, following the principles of the common law, would protect individuals from executive government.

These same beliefs were held in the former British colonies, such as Canada, New Zealand and Australia, even when they had written Constitutions which limited what their Parliaments could do in other ways. And Australia has kept these beliefs ever since, even though Canada and New Zealand now give special protection to rights. Britain may give special protection to rights, soon, too, if it agrees to make the European Convention on Human Rights part of British law.

Although Australia has no general Bill of Rights, the Australian Constitution puts some limits on government which work in a way very like a guarantee of particular rights. The protection which the Constitution gives to political speech and communication was mentioned in Chapter 13. The High Court has said that this is necessary in order to have a Parliament which is "directly chosen by the people..." A right to vote might be found in the same way, although this is far from sure.

The Constitution also puts a few other limits on government in ways which directly benefit individuals. These are described in the rest of this chapter.

Compensation for acquisition of property

Laws made by Parliament can affect people's rights, unless there is something in the Constitution to stop it.

One important right is the right to own property. There may be all sorts of reasons why a Parliament might want to pass a law to take someone's property, or to authorise someone else to take it. For example, the government might want to build a new road or to make a national park in areas where individuals own property.

Section 51(31) of the Constitution makes it clear that the Commonwealth Parliament can take or "acquire" property for any purpose for which it can make laws. Section 51 lists most of the Commonwealth's law-making powers. The Parliament can take property for any of these. For example, the Commonwealth can make laws for air travel under the interstate and overseas trade and commerce power in section 51(1) and the external affairs power in section 51(29). This means that it can use its power over property to take land to make a new airport, or to allow someone else to take the land. Importantly, however, the section also says that property must be acquired on "just terms". In other words, a person whose property is taken has a right to compensation which is reasonable and fair in the circumstances. This means that they will be given something (usually, money) in exchange for their property.

The right to be given compensation obviously applies to the taking of houses or land. But it applies when other kinds of property are taken as well: for example, the right to publish a book or a song (copyright) or the machinery which a person uses to run her business.

If the Commonwealth takes property of any kind for its own use, there is no doubt that it must pay compensation. But a Commonwealth law which just stops someone using their property for a particular purpose probably is not an "acquisition" which requires compensation to be paid. This was the case with the Commonwealth Act which prevented the Tasmanian government building the Franklin River dam in 1983. The Act did not "acquire" property within the meaning of this section.

Not all takings of property by government in Australia are covered by this rule. There is no constitutional requirement for the States to pay compensation when they take property (although they usually do). A suggestion that this and the other constitutional guarantees discussed in this chapter should be extended to the States was rejected at referendum in 1988.

Trial by jury

Trial by jury is a way of involving the community more widely in delivering justice. Historically, it was particularly important in criminal cases, where someone has been charged with a crime of some kind (for example, murder or stealing). The final decision about whether someone was guilty or not was made by 12 people (the jury) from the community whose laws the accused person was said to have broken. A person could only to found guilty if it was "beyond reasonable doubt". In that way, the jury applied the standards of the community.

Trial by jury sometimes is criticised in particular cases. If a case has attracted a lot of media attention (like the O.J. Simpson trial in the United States, for example), it may be hard to find people to be members of a jury who have not already made up their minds. A jury may find it hard to understand the facts of some cases, particularly where they involve complicated business dealings, such as a transfer of money between several different companies. Even so, trial by jury has been very important in our system of criminal justice and it still makes an important link between the law and the community.

Trial by jury gets some protection from the Australian Constitution although not very much. Section 80 says that "The trial on indictment of any offence against any law of the Commonwealth" must be "by jury". An indictment is one way of beginning a criminal case. It involves information about the offence being given to the court by the Attorney-General or someone else authorised to do this. The procedure of indictment is usually used to get more serious cases to trial.

Obviously, it is reasonable that serious cases should be tried by jury. But there is nothing in the Constitution to say that serious cases must be tried "on indictment". When it creates a new offence by passing a law which, if broken, will make something illegal, the Commonwealth Parliament can choose how someone should be accused of breaking the new law. It does not have to choose "trial on indictment". But according to the words of the Constitution, if a case does not begin with an "indictment", a jury is not required at all.

One way of working out whether a crime is serious or not, is to look at the type of punishment set out for it. A crime for which you could be put in gaol for 12 months is usually thought to be serious enough to require trial on indictment, with a jury. Some High Court judges have suggested that if the Commonwealth Parliament made a really serious offence (for example, one which allowed you to be put in gaol for two years), without saying that it had to be tried on indictment, section 80 might apply anyway, so that a jury would be needed.

The High Court has also said some other things about how section 80 works. All members of the jury have to agree, before someone can be found guilty of an offence. And because the section is important to the way in which our justice system works, people who are tried on indictment against the law of the Commonwealth must have a jury, whether they want to or not.

Section 80 only applies to offences against Commonwealth law. The Constitution does not make a jury necessary for serious offences against State law, although juries are often used in these cases.

Freedom of religion

The one traditional civil right which the Constitution clearly protects is freedom of religion. The section which deals with this is section 116. It sets out four separate rules. It stops the Commonwealth from "establishing" a national religion or, in other words, giving a special position to any one religion or branch of a religion. It stops the Commonwealth from requiring any religious observance (say, requiring everyone to promise in the name of God that they will tell the truth, when they speak in a court). It stops the Commonwealth from saying that people can't follow their own religious practices. And it stops the Commonwealth setting any religious test as a qualification for public office (it could not say that no-one who was a Roman Catholic could be a judge, for example). The section does not affect what the States can do, however.

Very few cases have been decided under section 116. This is partly because the Commonwealth does not have many powers which would let it make laws about religion anyway. But it does have some. The Commonwealth can't use any of them in a way which would give one religion an advantage over another or would give an advantage to religion generally.

Australians have many beliefs of different kinds. There is an important question about which of them are "religions" for the purposes of this section. The High Court has said that religion means any faith or belief, at least where it involves a "supernatural" being and uses set rituals or practices. It has also said, however, that the protection which the section gives to religion does not prevent the Commonwealth from making laws which are necessary for modern society. So, for example, section 116 does not prevent the Commonwealth from making laws about divorce, even though some religious beliefs disagree with divorce.

Interstate discrimination

There is no right to equality under the Australian Constitution and no general ban on discrimination. One particular kind of discrimination is banned, however. Section 117 stops discrimination against someone because he or she is a resident of another State. In other words, Tasmanians who go to New South Wales cannot be treated worse in New South Wales than residents of New South Wales in their position.

Section 117 has been noted before, in Chapter 5. The point made there is that the section describes the people it protects as "subjects of the

Queen". Whatever else these words mean nowadays, they certainly include Australian citizens.

There are three more points about the section which it is important to make as well.

The first is that section 117 does not say which government it applies to. In fact, the States are more likely to discriminate against residents of other States than the Commonwealth is. There is no doubt that the section applies to the States. It is possible that it applies to the Commonwealth too.

The section point concerns the effect of section 117. A law which discriminates against someone in a way which the section does not allow is still a law. It simply does not apply to the person who suffers from the discrimination. Other people will have to obey the law, unless it discriminates against them in the same unconstitutional way.

Thirdly, as with many constitutional guarantees, the prohibition in section 117 is not total and may not apply in some circumstances. The States exist for the purpose of governing State communities. The High Court has said that it is sometimes important for States to single out their own residents even though, when they do this, they will discriminate against others. Most obviously, a State is allowed to say that only its own residents can vote in State elections (as long it doesn't take too long to become a "resident"). And there may well be other examples of this as well.

A Bill of Rights for Australia?

No Parliament has total power in Australia. All parliaments must work within the guidelines set by the Constitution as interpreted and applied by the Courts unless and until the Constitution is changed with the approval of the Australian people.

The Constitution already limits the powers of Australian Parliaments, in all sorts of ways. It divides powers between them for the purposes of the federal system. It stops the Commonwealth Parliament having power which is "judicial" and can be used only by courts. As we will see in the next chapter, in order to set up a national economic system, it puts limits on what both the Commonwealth and the States Parliaments can do. And it puts a few other limits on the power of the Parliaments as well, which protect the rights of individuals in the ways already described.

From time to time the question is asked whether the Australian Constitution should protect other rights, or even have a Bill of Rights. So far, the answer has been no. It is possible that this debate might begin again, however. Australia is a more diverse community than it once was. Some of the delegates elected to the 1998 Constitutional Convention to discuss a republic also campaigned for better constitutional protection of rights. The idea that some rights should have special protection is accepted in many other countries and within the international community.

Democracy relies on majority decision-making in most if not all matters. Democracy also values individuals, however. We all agree that there are things in a democracy which a majority should not do. The main question is how to make sure that this happens. Can we continue to rely, as we have done in the past, on elected representatives in Parliaments? If so, are any changes needed to the parliamentary system to make it work as we want? Or should the Constitution limit what the majority can do, by referring to generally recognised standards, which have a lasting quality about them?

If we wanted a Bill of Rights, the experience of other countries shows that there are many different forms which it might take. There would be an important question, of course, about the rights to be stated in it. But there would be other questions as well. Should courts interpret and enforce a Bill of Rights? (We would be likely to use the courts, but some countries use other bodies: for example, their Parliaments.) Should a Bill of Rights list exceptions to particular rights (for example, freedom of speech but not freedom to encourage violence)? Should a Bill of Rights say that Parliaments can limit rights in the interests of the community, within particular guidelines as is done, for example, in South Africa? Should it even allow Parliaments to overrule particular rights for a fixed period (say, five years) as the Canadian Charter does? These options put limits of different kinds on what the majority can do. If and when protection of rights is discussed in Australia again it might be helpful to consider these options too.

26

Making a nation

Economic limits

The Constitution puts economic limits on government in Australia. The original purpose of these limits was to make sure that Australians would have a national economy after federation and that Australians would be able to move freely around all parts of the country.

Before federation Australia was six separate colonies, as we have mentioned before. Each colony had its own economy, as well as its own Constitution, system of government and laws. Different governments had different economic policies. Some, for example, believed in free trade. This meant that their industries would compete freely with those in other colonies or in other countries. Others thought that they would do better through "protection" or, in other words, giving special advantages to their local businesses. Each colony put taxes, or customs duties, on goods coming in from other Australian colonies: you can still see some of the old customs houses along State borders. The colonies had a small population and were a long way from the rest of the world. The economic divisions between them made things even harder for Australian farmers and Australian businesses.

One of the main reasons for federation in 1901 was the economic advantages it was expected to bring. Those advantages depended on setting up a single national market within Australia. This meant, for example, that the States would have to stop taxing each other's goods and competing with each other in ways which made most people worse off. On the other hand, it was important not to stop the States building up their economies in other ways. The very idea of a federal system is to bring different parts of the country together for some purposes, while leaving them with enough independence to make good use of their natural advantages and the energy of their own communities.

The challenge for the Constitutional Conventions of the 1890s was to decide what a Constitution could do to help to achieve these aims. The way in which that challenge was met is the subject of the rest of this chapter.

Going over old ground

Some of the answers lie in parts of the Constitution which have been discussed in earlier chapters.

It was quite easy to stop the States taxing each other's goods at the border. Section 90 gave the Commonwealth exclusive power to impose duties of customs. This meant that the States couldn't use these taxes at all.

Giving customs duties exclusively to the Commonwealth was useful for one other reason as well. It meant that taxes on goods from other countries would be the same for the whole of Australia. It would be up to the Commonwealth government and Parliament to decide whether those taxes should be set at a high level, so as to make overseas goods more expensive and encourage people to buy the cheaper Australian goods. Whatever decision they made, however, it would apply to all parts of Australia.

As we saw in Chapter 21, section 90 gives the Commonwealth exclusive power to impose duties of excise as well. This stops the States putting taxes on goods, even inside their own State. It means that they need to be given more money, or grants, by the Commonwealth. On the other hand, it also means that sales taxes are the same in all parts of Australia. This makes it easier for people who buy and sell things. And it makes it more difficult for someone to avoid paying sales tax by, for example, crossing the border into another State.

A national market also means that the most important laws dealing with the economy and with business should be the same in all parts of Australia. Most obviously, it was important for the money to be the same. This was easy enough to do as well. Section 51(12) gives the Commonwealth power over "currency and coinage". And section 115 stops the States from coining money at all.

The Constitution also made uniform laws possible in other areas, through the powers which it gave to the Commonwealth. If you look at the list of powers in section 51, you will see that almost half of them deal with economic or commercial matters: trade and commerce with other countries and between the States; banking; insurance; weights and measures; bills of exchange; bankruptcy; copyrights; trading corporations and industrial disputes are some of the most important.

Freedom of trade

All of these sections were needed for the kind of economic union which the framers had in mind, but they were not enough. They would not necessarily stop the States from protecting their own industries in other ways and so making the new national market less effective. For example, a State which made wine could set a limit, or quota, on the amount of wine which could be brought in from another State, so that its own wine-makers could charge more. Or a State which wanted to give extra help to its dairy industry could say that milk brought in from other States had to meet very high standards, to try to make it more expensive or to put people off bringing milk in at all.

The problem for the framers of the Constitution was to find the right words to stop these practices. Protection can take many different forms, and some are worse than others. It was not possible to think of them all, so as to list them in the Constitution. The framers needed some general words which would have the right effect.

The words which they finally chose are in the now famous section 92: "Trade, commerce and intercourse among the States shall be absolutely free". But the difficulty now was that the words were too general. Trade and commerce between the States could not in fact be absolutely free. For example, there is no reason why the Constitution should allow illegal guns to be carried from State to State, or encourage plant diseases to sweep the country.

Section 92 has led to more arguments about whether laws agree with the Constitution than any other section. The job of saying what it means belongs to the High Court. And the court has changed its mind over the years. This was mentioned in Chapter 14, to show how an interpretation by the High Court can change the meaning of the Constitution.

The present interpretation of section 92 was given in the following way. In 1988, in a case called *Cole v Whitfield*, the High Court was asked to decide whether a Tasmanian law which stopped people from having crayfish below a certain size could apply to someone in Tasmania who had bought their crayfish from South Australia where you are allowed to catch smaller crayfish. The High Court said that section 92 meant that laws could not discriminate against interstate trade in a way which protects the trade of a particular State. The Tasmanian law was legal, however. It did not give special advantages to the Tasmanian crayfish industry in a way which section 92 was intended to stop. Anyway, it had a worthwhile purpose of conserving Tasmanian crayfish stocks. The Court agreed, on the information given to it, that this could not be done in any other way.

The meaning which the High Court gave section 92 is clear enough, but some other questions have arisen under it. One, which the High Court has begun to tackle, is the effect of section 92 on a State law which appears to put in place a desirable policy (for example, environmental protection), but happens to protect the State's own industries as well. Another is how much the States can encourage local industries under section 92 as it is now interpreted. The answer to this last question is important for the balance between national unity and the ability of the States to assist their own communities.

The Interstate Commission

Despite the general wording of section 92, the framers of the Constitution still were not satisfied that it would create the kind of economic union which they wanted.

Sections 101 to 104 therefore provided for a special body to be set up, called the Interstate Commission, as a watchdog over the parts of the Constitution dealing with trade and commerce.

If you look at these sections, you will see that the Interstate Commission was expected to have a particular role in relation to interstate railways. This is because a common form of protection in the 1890s was for one colony to reduce its railway freight rates to encourage producers in another colony to use its ports. The sections also let the Interstate Commission be given other powers as well.

In fact, however, as we saw in Chapter 24 the Commission has not been important in the Australian federal system. In 1915 the High Court said that the Commission could not use judicial power because it was not a court. This meant that the Commission could not make decisions about whether a State was acting in a way which did not agree with section 92.

It has sometimes been suggested that the Commission could still have been useful for working out the effect of some State policies on freedom of trade, so as to help the High Court to make decisions under section 92. But it seems to be too late for that now. Although section 101 says that "there shall be an Interstate Commission", there isn't one. Whatever the Constitution says, there cannot be an Interstate Commission unless the Commonwealth Parliament sets it up and gives it money and the Commonwealth government appoints members to it. The story of the Interstate Commission shows that, while Constitutions are important, there are limits to what they can do.

Moving around Australia

The limits on government discussed in this chapter so far are supposed to make sure that businesses can operate in all parts of Australia and that goods can move freely around Australia.

But the creation of the Australian nation was important for more than trade and commerce. It was meant to have other benefits for Australians as well. It was hard to describe those benefits in the Constitution in 1901, before the idea of Australian citizenship developed. But at the very least, it was possible to say that federation meant that the Australian people could move around Australia too.

Two sections made sure that this happened. One is section 117, which was mentioned in the last chapter. It made it easier for Australians to move from State to State, by stopping discrimination against someone because of the State in which they happened to live.

The other section is section 92. Section 92 protects freedom of "intercourse" as well as trade and commerce among the States. Intercourse means movement of any kind across State borders, whether for commercial purposes or not. If you drive from Sydney to Perth, for example, you are involved in interstate intercourse. Section 92 protects your freedom to do this. No doubt there are limits to this freedom as well, to protect the community as a whole. The police would be able to stop you, for example, if you were driving a stolen car, or driving too fast. These sections are still important, however. We take these rights to move around for granted, but they helped to make Australia a nation, in 1901.

The Commonwealth and economic union

The rules in sections 92 and 117 most obviously put limits on what the States can do. A State is more likely to want to protect its own industries and to give special advantages to its own people than the Commonwealth is.

But the framers of the Constitution did not want the Commonwealth to play favourites between the States either. They probably expected that Commonwealth laws would always be the same in every State, unless there was a good reason why not, but they did not make this a rule. In commercial matters, however, the Constitution does limit the way in which the Commonwealth can use its power. The customs and excise duties which the Commonwealth has exclusive power to set must be the same, or uniform in all States. The Commonwealth has exclusive power to make payments, or bounties, to encourage Australian manufacturers, by paying them for each item they make here. But these bounties must be uniform too, under section 51(3). The Commonwealth cannot impose any kind of taxation in a way which discriminates between States or parts of States. Under section 99, the Commonwealth cannot give preference to any State or part of a State in any law or regulation of trade, commerce or revenue.

Neither section 92 nor section 117 say that they apply only to the States. It is unlikely that the Commonwealth would be tempted to act in a way which does not agree with either of them. Just in case, however, the High Court has said that the Commonwealth has to obey section 92. And while there has not been such a clear statement from the Court about section 117, it probably applies to the Commonwealth as well.

Mutual recognition

Most of the economic statements in the Australian Constitution protect the national market by stopping something from happening. They stop State governments giving special privileges to their own industries for their own goods. They stop the Commonwealth favouring one State over another.

The powers which the Constitution give to the Commonwealth Parliament positively encourage a national market because they make it more likely that the most important laws which affect business will be the same in all parts of Australia. But there are many State powers which can affect the national market as well. The States make laws about labelling and packaging of goods, for example, such as the warnings which must be put on cigarette packets. Most of the laws which set out standards for particular jobs are made by the States as well. For example, there are certain standards that people must meet to be electricians or doctors or teachers. When these laws are different as they often are, it is harder to do business in different States.

In the early 1990s, the States began to work together to deal with this problem. The agreement which they made is called Mutual Recognition. Mutual recognition makes each State accept each other's standards for goods and occupations. For example, Victorian eggs which meet Victorian standards can be sold in all other States, whatever the standards in those States may be. In the same way, someone who is allowed to work as a nurse in Queensland, or a builder in South Australia, or a real estate agent in Tasmania can work in the same job in the other States as well. The scheme is set up by Commonwealth legislation, using a reference of power from State Parliaments under section 51(37). This is important, because it means that the Commonwealth Act overrules any State laws which say something different.

As you might expect, some goods and occupations are left out of this scheme. The scheme also provides methods for dealing with arguments between government about particular standards. All the same, mutual recognition is an important development of the economic union which the Constitution was designed to create.

27

The Constitution turns one hundred

The past one hundred years

On 1 January 2001, the Australian Constitution will have been in use for exactly one hundred years.

During that time, it has done a good job. Its greatest achievement was to bring together the six Australian Colonies in a federation which is workable and which has lasted, despite occasional problems. The form of the Constitution has been flexible enough to adapt itself to very great changes in Australia's circumstances, including the move from colony to full independence. The Constitution has the distinction of a direct link with the Australian people, both in the way in which it was first made, and in the way in which it is changed now.

The Australian system of government, for which the Constitution provides the framework, has been admirable in other ways during this time. Australia has had a stable democracy, in which governments change from time to time, with little fuss. Australia sometimes has taken a lead in working out ways to improve democracy, which have been followed in other countries. Votes for women and the idea that you should be able to vote for your representatives in private (the secret ballot) are important examples, from earlier times. Generally, the rights and freedoms of individuals are respected. Australians are so used to the idea that the law should be obeyed that the rule of law is taken for granted.

How much of this is because of the Constitution is another question. The principles of parliamentary government and the rule of law were built into the Australian approach to government from colonial times. They were helped by the traditional down-to-earth Australian character, with its ideas about equality and a fair go. Despite wars and at least one major depression, neither democracy nor the rule of law has faced serious challenge. For its whole national history, Australia has had a very small population for its geographic size. Australians are well-off by world standards. Until recently, Australians have been able to treat their society as a largely homogenous or similar one, with a common language, common standards, common traditions. Democracy and the rule of law should have worked here, if they have worked anywhere.

In fact, the Australian Constitution says little about democracy. It sets out only three main requirements. One is that the House of Representatives must be elected every three years. The second is that the House and the Senate must be directly chosen by the people. The third is that the number of Members of the House of Representatives for each State must be in proportion to the numbers of the people of each State. The need for all Ministers to be Members of Parliament in section 64 may be a fourth. In all other major ways, possibly including the right to vote itself, Australians rely largely on legislation or the common law, rather than on the Constitution, for their democratic system.

The rule of law has more constitutional protection. For example, only courts can use judicial power. The power of the High Court to decide whether the government has broken the law cannot be removed without a referendum. The Constitution protects only the *need* to obey the law and the ways in which it is applied and enforced, however. It does not set standards for what the law says. We rely on Parliament for that.

The High Court added to the constitutional framework for Australian democracy, when it said that the requirement for the Houses of Parliament to be elected meant that Australians should be able to speak freely about political matters. A lot of argument and discussion followed these decisions. Both the decisions and the discussion which followed them have served the very practical purpose of drawing attention to the gaps in what the Constitution says about Australian democracy.

The next one hundred years

If the Constitution has worked so well over the past one hundred years, do these gaps matter? Maybe not. Certainly, we would not want to put so much detail in the Constitution that we can't experiment with ways which would improve our system of government further. On the other hand, at the end of the 20th century, it is a little odd for a Constitution to say as little as ours about the relations between people and their elected representatives. This is no reflection on the framers of the Constitution. Their main job was to make a federation and that was difficult enough.

Nor should we exaggerate the success of our democracy now or in the past. Most obviously, many Aboriginal Australians are likely to have mixed feelings about it. In Australia, as in many other countries, there seems to be an increasing lack of respect for or trust in elected representatives, which is not healthy for any democracy. Of course our democracy has its strengths, but we should recognise its weaknesses too.

By their very nature, Constitutions are meant to last. This means that they should not be changed easily, or without much thought. This is one reason why constitutions are written in general terms, the meaning of which develops gradually, or evolves, to meet changing circumstances. By and large, this has been the story of the Australian Constitution, although a few specific changes have been made.

On the other hand, the purpose of a Constitution is to provide a framework for a system of government and protection for its most important principles and rules. At some point evolution of a system of government is likely to run up against the words of a Constitution. On one view, the debate on the republic is an example of this. Australia's relationship with Britain has changed a lot over the last 100 years. If the next step in that development is for Australia to have its own Head of State, however, it cannot be done without changing the Constitution, because the role of the Queen is written in to it. At some point also, evolution takes the practice of government so far from the words of the Constitution that the Constitution itself becomes unimportant. And at some point the circumstances of a community change so much that some parts of the Constitution no longer work well and new rules are needed.

Whether the Australian Constitution has reached any of these points is a matter for Australians to decide. The centenary of the Constitution is a good time to think about these things. But while the centenary is a good opportunity it is not a deadline. It is more important for Australians to understand the real issues for the design of their system of government into the 21st century than to hurry these decisions through. If we try, we can build on the work of the framers of the original Constitution and leave some new constitutional traditions of which future Australians can be proud.

Commonwealth of Australia Constitution Act

(63 & 64 VICTORIA, CHAPTER 12)

An Act to constitute the Commonwealth of Australia.

[9th July 1900]

WHEREAS the people of New South Wales, Victoria, South Australia, Queensland, and Tasmania, humbly relying on the blessing of Almighty God, have agreed to unite in one indissoluble Federal Commonwealth under the Crown of the United Kingdom of Great Britain and Ireland, and under the Constitution hereby established:

And whereas it is expedient to provide for the admission into the Commonwealth of other Australasian Colonies and possessions of the Queen:

Be it therefore enacted by the Queen's most Excellent Majesty, by and with the advice and consent of the Lords Spiritual and Temporal, and Commons, in this present Parliament assembled, and by the authority of the same, as follows: −

1. Short title This Act may be cited as the Commonwealth of Australia Constitution Act.

2. Act to extend to the Queen's successors The provisions of this Act referring to the Queen shall extend to Her Majesty's heirs and successors in the sovereignty of the United Kingdom.

3. Proclamation of Commonwealth It shall be lawful for the Queen, with the advice of the Privy Council, to declare by proclamation that, on and after a day therein appointed, not being later than one year after the passing of this Act, the people of New South Wales, Victoria, South Australia, Queensland, and Tasmania, and also, if Her Majesty is satisfied that the people of Western Australia have agreed thereto, of Western Australia, shall be united in a Federal Commonwealth under the name of the Commonwealth of Australia. But the Queen may, at any time after the proclamation, appoint a Governor-General for the Commonwealth.

4. Commencement of Act The Commonwealth shall be established, and the Constitution of the Commonwealth shall take effect, on and after the day so appointed. But the Parliaments of the several colonies may at any time after the passing of this Act make any such laws, to come into operation on the day so appointed, as they might have made if the Constitution had taken effect at the passing of this Act.

5. Operation of the constitution and laws This Act, and all laws made by the Parliament of the Commonwealth under the Constitution, shall be binding on the courts, judges, and people of every State and of every part of the Commonwealth, notwithstanding anything in the laws of any State; and the laws of the Commonwealth shall be in force on all British ships, the Queen's ships of war excepted, whose first port of clearance and whose port of destination are in the Commonwealth.

6. Definitions "The Commonwealth" shall mean the Commonwealth of Australia as established under this Act.

"The States" shall mean such of the colonies of New South Wales, New Zealand, Queensland, Tasmania, Victoria, Western Australia, and South Australia, including the northern territory of South Australia, as for the time being are parts of the Commonwealth, and such colonies or territories as may be admitted into or established by the Commonwealth as States; and each of such parts of the Commonwealth shall be called "a State."

"Original States" shall mean such States as are parts of the Commonwealth at its establishment.

7. Repeal of Federal Council Act 48 & 49 Vict c 60 The Federal Council of Australasia Act, 1885, is hereby repealed, but so as not to affect any laws passed by the Federal Council of Australasia and in force at the establishment of the Commonwealth.

Any such law may be repealed as to any State by the Parliament of the Commonwealth, or as to any colony not being a State by the Parliament thereof.

8. Application of Colonial Boundaries Act 58 & 59 Vict c 34 After the passing of this Act the Colonial Boundaries Act, 1895, shall not apply to any colony which becomes a State of the Commonwealth; but the Commonwealth shall be taken to be a self-governing colony for the purposes of that Act.

9. Constitution The Constitution of the Commonwealth shall be as follows: –

THE CONSTITUTION.

CHAPTER 1.

THE PARLIAMENT.

PART 1. — GENERAL.

1. Legislative Power The legislative power of the Commonwealth shall be vested in a Federal Parliament, which shall consist of the Queen, a Senate, and a House of Representatives, and which is herein-after called "The Parliament," or "The Parliament of the Commonwealth."

2. Governor-General A Governor-General appointed by the Queen shall be Her Majesty's representative in the Commonwealth, and shall have and may exercise in the Commonwealth during the Queen's pleasure, but subject to this Constitution, such powers and functions of the Queen as Her Majesty may be pleased to assign to him.

3. Salary of Governor-General There shall be payable to the Queen out of the Consolidated Revenue fund of the Commonwealth, for the salary of the Governor-General, an annual sum which, until the Parliament otherwise provides, shall be ten thousand pounds.

The salary of a Governor-General shall not be altered during his continuance in office.

4. Provisions relating to Governor-General The provisions of this Constitution relating to the Governor-General extend and apply to the Governor-General for the time being, or such person as the Queen may appoint to administer the Government of the Commonwealth; but no such person shall be entitled to receive any salary from the Commonwealth in respect of any other office during his administration of the Government of the Commonwealth.

5. Sessions of Parliament. Prorogation and dissolution The Governor-General may appoint such times for holding the sessions of the Parliament as he thinks fit, and may also from time to time, by Proclamation or otherwise, prorogue the Parliament, and may in like manner dissolve the House of Representatives.

After any general election the Parliament shall be summoned to meet not later than thirty days after the day appointed for the return of the writs.

The Parliament shall be summoned to meet not later than six months after the establishment of the Commonwealth.

6. Yearly session of Parliament There shall be a session of the Parliament once at least in every year, so that twelve months shall not intervene between the last sitting of the Parliament in one session and its first sitting in the next session.

PART 2. — THE SENATE.

7. The Senate The Senate shall be composed of senators for each State, directly chosen by the people of the State, voting, until the Parliament otherwise provides, as one electorate.

But until the Parliament of the Commonwealth otherwise provides, the Parliament of the State of Queensland, if that State be an Original State, may make laws dividing the State into divisions and determining the number of senators to be chosen for each division, and in the absence of such provision the State shall be one electorate.

Until the Parliament otherwise provides there shall be six senators for each Original State. The Parliament may make laws increasing or diminishing the number of senators for each State, but so that equal representation of the several Original States shall be maintained and that no Original State shall have less than six senators.

The senators shall be chosen for a term of six years, and the names of the senators chosen for each State shall be certified by the Governor to the Governor-General.

8. Qualification of electors The qualification of electors of senators shall be in each State that which is prescribed by this Constitution, or by the Parliament, as the qualification for electors of members of the House of Representatives; but in the choosing of senators each elector shall vote only once.

9. Method of election of senators The Parliament of the Commonwealth may make laws prescribing the method of choosing senators, but so that the method shall be uniform for all States. Subject to any such law, the Parliament of each State may make laws prescribing the method of choosing the senators for that State.

Times and places The Parliament of a State may make laws for determining the times and places of elections of senators for the State.

10. Application of State laws Until the Parliament otherwise provides, but subject to this Constitution, the laws in force in each State, for the time being, relating to elections for the more numerous House of the Parliament of the State shall, as nearly as practicable, apply to elections of senators for the State.

11. Failure to choose senators The Senate may proceed to the despatch of business, notwithstanding the failure of any State to provide for its representation in the Senate.

12. Issue of writs The Governor of any State may cause writs to be issued for elections of senators for the State. In case of the dissolution of the Senate the writs shall be issued within ten days from the proclamation of such dissolution.

13. Rotation of senators [altered by No 1, 1907, s 2] As soon as may be after the Senate first meets, and after each first meeting of the Senate following a dissolution thereof, the Senate shall divide the senators chosen for each State into two classes, as nearly equal in number as practicable; and the places of the senators of the first class shall become vacant at the expiration of ~~the third year~~ **three years,** and the places of those of the second class at the expiration of ~~the sixth year~~ **six years,** from the beginning of their term of service; and afterwards the places of senators shall become vacant at the expiration of six years from the beginning of their term of service.

The election to fill vacant places shall be made ~~in the year at the expiration of which~~ **within one year before** the places are to become vacant.

For the purposes of this section the term of service of a senator shall be taken to begin on the first day of ~~January~~ **July** following the day of his election, except in the cases of the first election and of the election next after any dissolution of the Senate, when it shall be taken to begin on the first day of ~~January~~ **July** preceding the day of his election.

14. Further provision for rotation Whenever the number of senators for a State is increased or diminished, the Parliament of the Commonwealth may make such provision for the vacating of the places of senators for the State as it deems necessary to maintain regularity in the rotation.

15. Casual vacancies [substituted by No 82, 1977, s 2] If the place of a senator becomes vacant before the expiration of his term of service, the Houses of Parliament of the State for which he was chosen, sitting and voting together, or, if there is only one House of that Parliament, that House, shall choose a person to hold the place until the expiration of the term. But if the Parliament of the State is not in session when the vacancy is notified, the Governor of the State, with the advice of the Executive Council thereof, may appoint a person to hold the place until the expiration of fourteen days from the beginning of the next session of the Parliament of the State or the expiration of the term, whichever first happens.

Where a vacancy has at any time occurred in the place of a senator chosen by the people of a State and, at the time when he was so chosen, he was publicly recognized by a particular political party as being an endorsed candidate of that party and publicly represented himself to be such a candidate, a person chosen or appointed under this section in consequence of that vacancy, or in consequence of that vacancy and a subsequent vacancy or vacancies, shall, unless there is no member of that party available to be chosen or appointed, be a member of that party.

Where –

(a) in accordance with the last preceding paragraph, a member of a particular political party is chosen or appointed to hold the place of a senator whose place had become vacant; and

(b) before taking his seat he ceases to be a member of that party (otherwise than by reason of the party having ceased to exist),

he shall be deemed not to have been so chosen or appointed and the vacancy shall be again notified in accordance with section twenty-one of this Constitution.

The name of any senator chosen or appointed under this section shall be certified by the Governor of the State to the Governor-General.

If the place of a senator chosen by the people of a State at the election of senators last held before the commencement of the *Constitution Alteration (Senate Casual Vacancies)* 1977 became vacant before that commencement and, at that commencement, no person chosen by the House or Houses of Parliament of the State, or appointed by the Governor of the State, in consequence of that vacancy, or in consequence of that vacancy and a subsequent vacancy or vacancies, held office, this section applies as if the place of the senator chosen by the people of the State had become vacant after that commencement.

A senator holding office at the commencement of the *Constitution Alteration (Senate Casual Vacancies)* 1977, being a senator appointed by the Governor of a State in consequence of a vacancy that had at any time occurred in the place of a senator chosen by the people of the State, shall be deemed to have been appointed to hold the place until the expiration of fourteen days after the beginning of the next session of the Parliament of the State that commenced or commences after he was appointed and further action under this section shall be taken as if the vacancy in the place of the senator chosen by the people of the State had occurred after that commencement.

Subject to the next succeeding paragraph, a senator holding office at the commencement of the *Constitution Alteration (Senate Casual Vacancies)* 1977 who was chosen by the House or Houses of Parliament of a State in consequence of a vacancy that had at any time occurred in the place of a senator chosen by the people of the State shall be deemed to have been chosen to hold office until the expiration of the term of service of the senator elected by the people of the State.

If, at or before the commencement of the *Constitution Alteration (Senate Casual Vacancies)* 1977, a law to alter the Constitution entitled "*Constitution Alteration (Simultaneous Elections)* 1977" came into operation, a senator holding office at the commencement of that law who was chosen by the House or Houses of Parliament of a State in consequence of a vacancy that had at any time occurred in the place of a Senator chosen by the people of the State shall be deemed to have been chosen to hold office —

(a) if the senator elected by the people of the State had a term of service expiring on the thirtieth day of June, One thousand nine hundred and seventy-eight—until the expiration or dissolution of the first House of Representatives to expire or be dissolved after that law came into operation; or

(b) if the senator elected by the people of the State had a term of service expiring on the thirtieth day of June, One thousand nine hundred and eighty-one—until the expiration or dissolution of the second House of Representatives to expire or be dissolved after that law came into operation or, if there is an earlier dissolution of the Senate, until that dissolution.

16. Qualifications of senator The qualifications of a senator shall be the same as those of a member of the House of Representatives.

17. Election of President The Senate shall, before proceeding to the despatch of any other business, choose a senator to be the President of the Senate; and as often as the office of President becomes vacant the Senate shall again choose a senator to be the President.

The President shall cease to hold his office if he ceases to be a senator. He may be removed from office by a vote of the Senate, or he may resign his office or his seat by writing addressed to the Governor-General.

18. Absence of President Before or during any absence of the President, the Senate may choose a senator to perform his duties in his absence.

19. Resignation of senator A senator may, by writing addressed to the President, or to the Governor-General if there is no President or if the President is absent from the Commonwealth, resign his place, which thereupon shall become vacant.

20. Vacancy by absence The place of a senator shall become vacant if for two consecutive months of any session of the Parliament he, without the permission of the Senate, fails to attend the Senate.

21. Vacancy to be notified Whenever a vacancy happens in the Senate, the President, or if there is no President or if the President is absent from the Commonwealth the Governor-General, shall notify the same to the Governor of the State in the representation of which the vacancy has happened.

22. Quorum Until the Parliament otherwise provides, the presence of at least one-third of the whole number of the senators shall be necessary to constitute a meeting of the Senate for the exercise of its powers.

23. Voting in the Senate Questions arising in the Senate shall be determined by a majority of votes, and each senator shall have one vote. The President shall in all cases be entitled to a vote; and when the votes are equal the question shall pass in the negative.

PART 3. — THE HOUSE OF REPRESENTATIVES.

24. Constitution of House of Representatives The House of Representatives shall be composed of members directly chosen by the people of the Commonwealth, and the number of such members shall be, as nearly as practicable, twice the number of the senators.

The number of members chosen in the several States shall be in proportion to the respective numbers of their people, and shall, until the Parliament otherwise provides, be determined, whenever necessary, in the following manner: –

(1.)   A quota shall be ascertained by dividing the number of the people of the Commonwealth, as shown by the latest statistics of the Commonwealth, by twice the number of the senators:

(2.)   The number of members to be chosen in each State shall be determined by dividing the number of the people of the State, as shown by the latest statistics of the Commonwealth, by the quota; and if on such division there is a remainder greater than one-half of the quota, one more member shall be chosen in the State.

But notwithstanding anything in this section, five members at least shall be chosen in each Original State.

25. Provision as to races disqualified from voting For the purposes of the last section, if by the law of any State all persons of any race are disqualified from voting at elections for the more numerous House of the Parliament of the State, then, in reckoning the number of the people of the State or of the Commonwealth, persons of that race resident in that State shall not be counted.

26. Representatives in first Parliament Notwithstanding anything in section twenty-four, the number of members to be chosen in each State at the first election shall be as follows: –

New South Wales .... twenty-three;

Victoria .... twenty;

Queensland .... eight;

South Australia.............. six;

Tasmania .... five;

Provided that if Western Australia is an Original State, the numbers shall be as follows: –

New South Wales .... twenty-six;

Victoria .... twenty-three;

Queensland.................... nine;

South Australia.............. seven;

Western Australia.......... five;

Tasmania .... five.

27. Alteration of number of members Subject to this Constitution, the Parliament may make laws for increasing or diminishing the number of the members of the House of Representatives.

28. Duration of House of Representatives Every House of Representatives shall continue for three years from the first meeting of the House, and no longer, but may be sooner dissolved by the Governor-General.

29. Electoral divisions Until the Parliament of the Commonwealth otherwise provides, the Parliament of any State may make laws for determining the divisions in each State for which members of the House of Representatives may be chosen, and the number of members to be chosen for each division. A division shall not be formed out of parts of different States.

In the absence of other provision, each State shall be one electorate.

30. Qualification of electors Until the Parliament otherwise provides, the qualification of electors of members of the House of Representatives shall be in each State that which is prescribed by the law of the State as the qualification of electors of the more numerous House of Parliament of the State; but in the choosing of members each elector shall vote only once.

31. Application of State laws Until the Parliament otherwise provides, but subject to this Constitution, the laws in force in each State for the time being relating to elections for the more numerous House of the Parliament of the State shall, as nearly as practicable, apply to elections in the State of members of the House of Representatives.

32. Writs for general election The Governor-General in Council may cause writs to be issued for general elections of members of the House of Representatives.

After the first general election, the writs shall be issued within ten days from the expiry of a House of Representatives or from the proclamation of a dissolution thereof.

33. Writs for vacancies Whenever a vacancy happens in the House of Representatives, the Speaker shall issue his writ for the election of a new member, or if there is no Speaker or if he is absent from the Commonwealth the Governor-General in Council may issue the writ.

34. Qualifications of members Until the Parliament otherwise provides, the qualifications of a member of the House of Representatives shall be as follows: –

(1.)   He must be of the full age of twenty-one years, and must be an elector entitled to vote at the election of members of the House of Representatives, or a person qualified to become such elector, and must have been for three years at the least a resident within the limits of the Commonwealth as existing at the time when he is chosen;

(2.)   He must be a subject of the Queen, either natural-born or for at least five years naturalized under a law of the United Kingdom, or of a Colony which has become or becomes a State, or of the Commonwealth, or of a State.

35. Election of speaker The House of Representatives shall, before proceeding to the despatch of any other business, choose a member to be the Speaker of the House, and as often as the office of Speaker becomes vacant the House shall again choose a member to be the Speaker.

The Speaker shall cease to hold his office if he ceases to be a member. He may be removed from office by a vote of the House, or he may resign his office or his seat by writing addressed to the Governor-General.

36. Absence of Speaker Before or during any absence of the Speaker, the House of Representatives may choose a member to perform his duties in his absence.

37. Resignation of member A member may by writing addressed to the Speaker, or to the Governor-General if there is no Speaker or if the Speaker is absent from the Commonwealth, resign his place, which thereupon shall become vacant.

38. Vacancy by absence The place of a member shall become vacant if for two consecutive months of any session of the Parliament he, without the permission of the House, fails to attend the House.

39. Quorum Until the Parliament otherwise provides, the presence of at least one-third of the whole number of the members of the House of Representatives shall be necessary to constitute a meeting of the House for the exercise of its powers.

40. Voting in House of Representatives Questions arising in the House of Representatives shall be determined by a majority of votes other than that of the Speaker. The Speaker shall not vote unless the numbers are equal, and then he shall have a casting vote.

PART 4. — BOTH HOUSES OF THE PARLIAMENT.

41. Right of electors of States No adult person who has or acquires a right to vote at elections for the more numerous House of the Parliament of a State shall, while the right continues, be prevented by any law of the Commonwealth from voting at elections for either House of the Parliament of the Commonwealth.

42. Oath or affirmation of allegiance Every senator and every member of the House of Representatives shall before taking his seat make and subscribe before the Governor-General, or some person authorised by him, an oath or affirmation of allegiance in the form set forth in the schedule to this Constitution.

43. Member of one House ineligible for other A member of either House of the Parliament shall be incapable of being chosen or of sitting as a member of the other House.

44. Disqualification Any person who –
- (1.)   Is under any acknowledgment of allegiance, obedience, or adherence to a foreign power, or is a subject or a citizen or entitled to the rights or privileges of a subject or a citizen of a foreign power: or
- (2.)   Is attainted of treason, or has been convicted and is under sentence, or subject to be sentenced, for any offence punishable under the law of the Commonwealth or of a State by imprisonment for one year or longer: or
- (3.)   Is an undischarged bankrupt or insolvent: or
- (4.)   Holds any office of profit under the Crown, or any pension payable during the pleasure of the Crown out of any of the revenues of the Commonwealth: or
- (5.)   Has any direct or indirect pecuniary interest in any agreement with the Public Service of the Commonwealth otherwise than as a member and in common with the other members of an incorporated company consisting of more than twenty-five persons:

shall be incapable of being chosen or of sitting as a senator or a member of the House of Representatives.

But sub-section iv. does not apply to the office of any of the Queen's Ministers of State for the Commonwealth, or of any of the Queen's Ministers for a State, or to the receipt of pay, half pay, or a pension, by any person as an officer or member of the Queen's navy or army, or to the receipt of pay as an officer or member of the naval or military forces of the Commonwealth by any person whose services are not wholly employed by the Commonwealth.

45. Vacancy on happening of disqualification If a senator or member of the House of Representatives –
- (1.)   Becomes subject to any of the disabilities mentioned in the last preceding section: or
- (2.)   Takes the benefit, whether by assignment, composition, or otherwise, of any law relating to bankrupt or insolvent debtors: or
- (3.)   Directly or indirectly takes or agrees to take any fee or honorarium for services rendered to the Commonwealth, or for services rendered in the Parliament to any person or State:

his place shall thereupon become vacant.

46. Penalty for sitting when disqualified Until the Parliament otherwise provides, any person declared by this Constitution to be incapable of sitting as a senator or as a member of the House of Representatives shall, for every day on which he so sits, be liable to pay the sum of one hundred pounds to any person who sues for it in any court of competent jurisdiction.

47. Disputed elections Until the Parliament otherwise provides, any question respecting the qualification of a senator or of a member of the House of Representatives, or respecting a vacancy in either House of the Parliament, and any question of a disputed election to either House, shall be determined by the House in which the question arises.

48. Allowance to members Until the Parliament otherwise provides, each senator and each member of the House of Representatives shall receive an allowance of four hundred pounds a year, to be reckoned from the day on which he takes his seat.

49. Privileges, &c of Houses The powers, privileges, and immunities of the Senate and of the House of Representatives, and of the members and the committees of each House, shall be such as are declared by the Parliament, and until declared shall be those of the Commons House of Parliament of the United Kingdom, and of its members and committees, at the establishment of the Commonwealth.

50. Rules and orders Each House of the Parliament may make rules and orders with respect to –

(1.)   The mode in which its powers, privileges, and immunities may be exercised and upheld:

(2.)   The order and conduct of its business and proceedings either separately or jointly with the other House.

PART 5. — POWERS OF THE PARLIAMENT.

51. Legislative powers of the Parliament The Parliament shall, subject to this Constitution, have power to make laws for the peace, order, and good government of the Commonwealth with respect to: –

(1.)   Trade and commerce with other countries, and among the States:

(2.)   Taxation; but so as not to discriminate between States or parts of States:

(3.)   Bounties on the production or export of goods, but so that such bounties shall be uniform throughout the Commonwealth:

(4.)   Borrowing money on the public credit of the Commonwealth:

(5.)   Postal, telegraphic, telephonic, and other like services:

(6.)   The naval and military defence of the Commonwealth and of the several States, and the control of the forces to execute and maintain the laws of the Commonwealth:

(7.)   Lighthouses, lightships, beacons and buoys:

(8.)   Astronomical and meteorological observations:

(9.)   Quarantine:

(10.)   Fisheries in Australian waters beyond territorial limits:

(11.)   Census and statistics:

(12.)   Currency, coinage, and legal tender:

(13.)   Banking, other than State banking; also State banking extending beyond the limits of the State concerned, the incorporation of banks, and the issue of paper money:

(14.)   Insurance, other than State insurance; also State insurance extending beyond the limits of the State concerned:

(15.)   Weights and measures:

(16.)   Bills of exchange and promissory notes:

(17.)   Bankruptcy and insolvency:

(18.)   Copyrights, patents of inventions and designs, and trade marks:

(19.)   Naturalization and aliens:

(20.)   Foreign corporations, and trading or financial corporations formed within the limits of the Commonwealth:

(21.)   Marriage;

(22.)   Divorce and matrimonial causes; and in relation thereto, parental rights, and the custody and guardianship of infants:

(23.)   Invalid and old-age pensions:

(23A.)   **[inserted by No 81, 1946, s 2]** The provision of maternity allowances, widows' pensions, child endowment, unemployment, pharmaceutical, sickness and hospital benefits, medical and dental services (but not so as to authorize any form of civil conscription), benefits to students and family allowances:

(24.)   The service and execution throughout the Commonwealth of the civil and criminal process and the judgments of the courts of the States:

(25.)   The recognition throughout the Commonwealth of the laws, the public Acts and records, and the judicial proceedings of the States:

(26.)   **[altered by No 55, 1967, s 2]** The people of any race, ~~other than the aboriginal race in any State,~~ for whom it is deemed necessary to make special laws:

(27.)   Immigration and emigration:

(28.)   The influx of criminals:

(29.)   External affairs:

(30.)   The relations of the Commonwealth with the islands of the Pacific:

(31.)   The acquisition of property on just terms from any State or person for any purpose in respect of which the Parliament has power to make laws:

(32.)   The control of railways with respect to transport for the naval and military purposes of the Commonwealth:

(33.)   The acquisition, with the consent of a State, of any railways of the State on terms arranged between the Commonwealth and the State:

(34.)   Railway construction and extension in any State with the consent of that State:

(35.)   Conciliation and arbitration for the prevention and settlement of industrial disputes extending beyond the limits of any one State:

(36.)   Matters in respect of which this Constitution makes provision until the Parliament otherwise provides:

(37.)   Matters referred to the Parliament of the Commonwealth by the Parliament or Parliaments of any State or States, but so that the law shall extend only to States by whose Parliaments the matter is referred, or which afterwards adopt the law:

(38.) The exercise within the Commonwealth, at the request or with the concurrence of the Parliaments of all the States directly concerned, of any power which can at the establishment of this Constitution be exercised only by the Parliament of the United Kingdom or by the Federal Council of Australasia:

(39.) Matters incidental to the execution of any power vested by this Constitution in the Parliament or in either House thereof, or in the Government of the Commonwealth, or in the Federal Judicature, or in any department or officer of the Commonwealth.

52. Exclusive powers of the Parliament The Parliament shall, subject to this Constitution, have exclusive power to make laws for the peace, order, and good government of the Commonwealth with respect to –

(1.) The seat of government of the Commonwealth, and all places acquired by the Commonwealth for public purposes:

(2.) Matters relating to any department of the public service the control of which is by this Constitution transferred to the Executive Government of the Commonwealth:

(3.) Other matters declared by this Constitution to be within the exclusive power of the Parliament.

53. Powers of the Houses in respect of legislation Proposed laws appropriating revenue or moneys, or imposing taxation, shall not originate in the Senate. But a proposed law shall not be taken to appropriate revenue or moneys, or to impose taxation, by reason only of its containing provisions for the imposition or appropriation of fines or other pecuniary penalties, or for the demand or payment or appropriation of fees for licenses, or fees for services under the proposed law.

The Senate may not amend proposed laws imposing taxation, or proposed laws appropriating revenue or moneys for the ordinary annual services of the Government.

The Senate may not amend any proposed law so as to increase any proposed charge or burden on the people.

The Senate may at any stage return to the House of Representatives any proposed law which the Senate may not amend, requesting, by message, the omission or amendment of any items or provisions therein. And the House of Representatives may, if it thinks fit, make any of such omissions or amendments, with or without modifications.

Except as provided in this section, the Senate shall have equal power with the House of Representatives in respect of all proposed laws.

54. Appropriation Bills The proposed law which appropriates revenue or moneys for the ordinary annual services of the Government shall deal only with such appropriation.

55. Tax Bill Laws imposing taxation shall deal only with the imposition of taxation, and any provision therein dealing with any other matter shall be of no effect.

Laws imposing taxation, except laws imposing duties of customs or of excise, shall deal with one subject of taxation only; but laws imposing duties of customs shall deal with duties of customs only, and laws imposing duties of excise shall deal with duties of excise only.

56. Recommendation of money votes A vote, resolution, or proposed law for the appropriation of revenue or moneys shall not be passed unless the purpose of the appropriation has in the same session been recommended by message of the Governor-General to the House in which the proposal originated.

57. Disagreement between the Houses If the House of Representatives passes any proposed law, and the Senate rejects or fails to pass it, or passes it with amendments to which the House of Representatives will not agree, and if after an interval of three months the House of Representatives, in the same or the next session, again passes the proposed law with or without any amendments which have been made, suggested, or agreed to by the Senate, and the Senate rejects or fails to pass it, or passes it with amendments to which the House of Representatives will not agree, the Governor-General may dissolve the Senate and the House of Representatives simultaneously. But such dissolution shall not take place within six months before the date of the expiry of the House of Representatives by effluxion of time.

If after such dissolution the House of Representatives again passes the proposed law, with or without any amendments which have been made, suggested, or agreed to by the Senate, and the Senate rejects or fails to pass it, or passes it with amendments to which the House of Representatives will not agree, the Governor-General may convene a joint sitting of the members of the Senate and of the House of Representatives.

The members present at the joint sitting may deliberate and shall vote together upon the proposed law as last proposed by the House of Representatives, and upon amendments, if any, which have been made therein by one House and not agreed to by the other, and any such amendments which are affirmed by an absolute majority of the total number of the members of the Senate and House of Representatives shall be taken to have been carried, and if the proposed law, with the amendments, if any, so carried is affirmed by an absolute majority of the total number of the members of the Senate and House of Representatives, it shall be taken to have been duly passed by both Houses of the Parliament, and shall be presented to the Governor-General for the Queen's assent.

58. Royal assent to Bills When a proposed law passed by both Houses of the Parliament is presented to the Governor-General for the Queen's assent, he shall declare, according to his discretion, but subject to this Constitution, that he assents in the Queen's name, or that he withholds assent, or that he reserves the law for the Queen's pleasure.

Recommendations by Governor-General The Governor-General may return to the house in which it originated any proposed law so presented to him, and may transmit therewith any amendments which he may recommend, and the Houses may deal with the recommendation.

59. Disallowance by the Queen The Queen may disallow any law within one year from the Governor-General's assent, and such disallowance on being made known by the Governor-General by speech or message to each of the Houses of the Parliament, or by Proclamation, shall annul the law from the day when the disallowance is so made known.

60. Signification of Queen's pleasure on Bills reserved A proposed law reserved for the Queen's pleasure shall not have any force unless and until within two years from the day on which it was presented to the Governor-General for the Queen's assent the Governor-General makes known, by speech or message to each of the Houses of the Parliament, or by Proclamation, that it has received the Queen's assent.

CHAPTER 2.

THE EXECUTIVE GOVERNMENT.

61. Executive power The executive power of the Commonwealth is vested in the Queen and is exercisable by the Governor-General as the Queen's representative, and extends to the execution and maintenance of this Constitution, and of the laws of the Commonwealth.

62. Federal Executive Council There shall be a Federal Executive Council to advise the Governor-General in the government of the Commonwealth, and the members of the Council shall be chosen and summoned by the Governor-General and sworn as Executive Councillors, and shall hold office during his pleasure.

63. Provisions referring to Governor-General The provisions of this Constitution referring to the Governor-General in Council shall be construed as referring to the Governor-General acting with the advice of the Federal Executive Council.

64. Ministers of State The Governor-General may appoint officers to administer such departments of State of the Commonwealth as the Governor-General in Council may establish.

Such officers shall hold office during the pleasure of the Governor-General. They shall be members of the Federal Executive Council, and shall be the Queen's Ministers of State for the Commonwealth.

Ministers to sit in Parliament After the first general election no Minister of State shall hold office for a longer period than three months unless he is or becomes a senator or a member of the House of Representatives.

65. Number of Ministers Until the Parliament otherwise provides, the Ministers of State shall not exceed seven in number, and shall hold such offices as the Parliament prescribes, or, in the absence of provision, as the Governor-General directs.

66. Salaries of Ministers There shall be payable to the Queen, out of the Consolidated Revenue Fund of the Commonwealth, for the salaries of the Ministers of State, an annual sum which, until the Parliament otherwise provides, shall not exceed twelve thousand pounds a year.

67. Appointment of civil servants Until the Parliament otherwise provides, the appointment and removal of all other officers of the Executive Government of the Commonwealth shall be vested in the Governor-General in Council, unless the appointment is delegated by the Governor-General in Council or by a law of the Commonwealth to some other authority.

68. Command of naval and military forces The command in chief of the naval and military forces of the Commonwealth is vested in the Governor-General as the Queen's representative.

69. Transfer of certain departments On a date or dates to be proclaimed by the Governor-General after the establishment of the Commonwealth the following departments of the public service in each State shall become transferred to the Commonwealth: –

Posts, telegraphs, and telephones:
Naval and military defence:
Lighthouses, lightships, beacons, and buoys:
Quarantine.

But the departments of customs and of excise in each State shall become transferred to the Commonwealth on its establishment.

70. Certain powers of Governors to vest in Governor-General In respect of matters which, under this Constitution, pass to the Executive Government of the Commonwealth, all powers and functions which at the establishment of the Commonwealth are vested in the Governor of a Colony, or in the Governor of a Colony with the advice of his Executive Council, or in any authority of a Colony, shall vest in the Governor-General, or in the Governor-General in Council, or in the authority exercising similar powers under the Commonwealth, as the case requires.

––––––––––

CHAPTER 3.

THE JUDICATURE.

71. Judicial power and Courts The judicial power of the Commonwealth shall be vested in a Federal Supreme Court, to be called the High Court of Australia, and in such other federal courts as the Parliament creates, and in such other courts as it invests with federal jurisdiction. The High Court shall consist of a Chief Justice, and so many other Justices, not less than two, as the Parliament prescribes.

72. Judges' appointment, tenure and remuneration The Justices of the High Court and of the other courts created by the Parliament –

(1.)   Shall be appointed by the Governor-General in Council:

(2.)   Shall not be removed except by the Governor-General in Council, on an address from both Houses of the Parliament in the same session, praying for such removal on the ground of proved misbehaviour or incapacity:

(3.)   Shall receive such remuneration as the Parliament may fix; but the remuneration shall not be diminished during their continuance in office.

[this and the following paragraphs added by No 83, 1977, s 2] The appointment of a Justice of the High Court shall before a term expiring upon his attaining the age of seventy years, and a person shall not be appointed as a Justice of the High Court if he has attained that age.

The appointment of a Justice of a court created by the Parliament shall be for a term expiring upon his attaining the age that is, at the time of his appointment, the maximum age for Justices of that court and a person shall not be appointed as a Justice of such a court if he has attained the age that is for the time being the maximum age for Justices of that court.

Subject to this section, the maximum age for Justices of any court created by the Parliament is seventy years.

The Parliament may make a law fixing an age that is less than seventy years as the maximum age for Justices of a court created by the Parliament and may at any time repeal or amend such a law, but any such repeal or amendment does not affect the term of office of a Justice under an appointment made before the repeal or amendment.

A Justice of the High Court or of a court created by the Parliament may resign his office by writing under his hand delivered to the Governor-General.

Nothing in the provisions added to this section by the *Constitution Alteration (Retirement of Judges) 1977* affects the continuance of a person in office as a Justice of a court under an appointment made before the commencement of those provisions.

A reference in this section to the appointment of a Justice of the High Court or of a court created by the Parliament shall be read as including a reference to the appointment of a person who holds office as a Justice of the High Court or of a court created by the Parliament to another office of Justice of the same court having a different status or designation.

73. Appellate jurisdiction of High Court The High Court shall have jurisdiction, with such exceptions and subject to such regulations as the Parliament prescribes, to hear and determine appeals from all judgments, decrees, orders, and sentences —

(1.) Of any Justice or Justices exercising the original jurisdiction of the High Court:

(2.) Of any other federal court, or court exercising federal jurisdiction; or of the Supreme Court of any State, or of any other court of any State from which at the establishment of the Commonwealth an appeal lies to the Queen in Council:

(3.) Of the Inter-State Commission, but as to questions of law only:

and the judgment of the High Court in all such cases shall be final and conclusive.

But no exception or regulation prescribed by the Parliament shall prevent the High Court from hearing and determining any appeal from the Supreme Court of a State in any matter in which at the establishment of the Commonwealth an appeal lies from such Supreme Court to the Queen in Council.

Until the Parliament otherwise provides, the conditions of and restrictions on appeals to the Queen in Council from the Supreme Courts of the several States shall be applicable to appeals from them to the High Court.

74. Appeal to Queen in Council No appeal shall be permitted to the Queen in Council from a decision of the High Court upon any question, howsoever arising, as to the limits inter se of the Constitutional powers of the Commonwealth and those of any State or States, or as to the limits inter se of the Constitutional powers of any two or more States, unless the High Court shall certify that the question is one which ought to be determined by Her Majesty in Council.

The High Court may so certify if satisfied that for any special reason the certificate should be granted, and thereupon an appeal shall lie to Her Majesty in Council on the question without further leave.

Except as provided in this section, this Constitution shall not impair any right which the Queen may be pleased to exercise by virtue of Her Royal prerogative to grant special leave of appeal from the High Court to Her Majesty in Council. The Parliament may make laws limiting the matters in which such leave may be asked, but proposed laws containing any such limitation shall be reserved by the Governor-General for Her Majesty's pleasure.

75. Original jurisdiction of High Court In all matters –
- (1.) Arising under any treaty:
- (2.) Affecting consuls or other representatives of other countries:
- (3.) In which the Commonwealth, or a person suing or being sued on behalf of the Commonwealth, is a party:
- (4.) Between States, or between residents of different States, or between a State and a resident of another State:
- (5.) In which a writ of Mandamus or prohibition or an injunction is sought against an officer of the Commonwealth:

the High Court shall have original jurisdiction.

76. Additional original jurisdiction The Parliament may make laws conferring original jurisdiction on the High Court in any matter –
- (1.) Arising under this Constitution, or involving its interpretation:
- (2.) Arising under any laws made by the Parliament:
- (3.) Of Admiralty and maritime jurisdiction:
- (4.) Relating to the same subject-matter claimed under the laws of different States.

77. Power to define jurisdiction With respect to any of the matters mentioned in the last two sections the Parliament may make laws –
- (1.) Defining the jurisdiction of any federal court other than the High Court:
- (2.) Defining the extent to which the jurisdiction of any federal court shall be exclusive of that which belongs to or is invested in the courts of the States:
- (3.) Investing any court of a State with federal jurisdiction.

78. Proceedings against Commonwealth or State The Parliament may make laws conferring rights to proceed against the Commonwealth or a State in respect of matters within the limits of the judicial power.

79. Number of judges The federal jurisdiction of any court may be exercised by such number of judges as the Parliament prescribes.

80. Trial by jury The trial on indictment of any offence against any law of the Commonwealth shall be by jury, and every such trial shall be held in the State where the offence was committed, and if the offence was not committed within any State the trial shall be held at such place or places as the Parliament prescribes.

CHAPTER 4.

FINANCE AND TRADE.

81. Consolidated Revenue Fund All revenue or moneys raised or received by the Executive Government of the Commonwealth shall form one Consolidated Revenue Fund, to be appropriated for the purposes of the Commonwealth in the manner and subject to the charges and liabilities imposed by this Constitution.

82. Expenditure charged thereon The costs, charges, and expenses incident to the collection, management, and receipt of the Consolidated Revenue Fund shall form the first charge thereon; and the revenue of the Commonwealth shall in the first instance be applied to the payment of the expenditure of the Commonwealth.

83. Money to be appropriated by law No money shall be drawn from the Treasury of the Commonwealth except under appropriation made by law.

But until the expiration of one month after the first meeting of the Parliament the Governor-General in Council may draw from the Treasury and expend such moneys as may be necessary for the maintenance of any department transferred to the Commonwealth and for the holding of the first elections for the Parliament.

84. Transfer of officers When any department of the public service of a State becomes transferred to the Commonwealth, all officers of the department shall become subject to the control of the Executive Government of the Commonwealth.

Any such officer who is not retained in the service of the Commonwealth shall, unless he is appointed to some other office of equal emolument in the public service of the State, be entitled to receive from the State any pension, gratuity, or other compensation, payable under the law of the State on the abolition of his office.

Any such officer who is retained in the service of the Commonwealth shall preserve all his existing and accruing rights, and shall be entitled to retire from office at the time, and on the pension or retiring allowance, which would be permitted by the law of the State if his service with the Commonwealth were a continuation of his service with the State. Such pension or retiring allowance shall be paid to him by the Commonwealth; but the State shall pay to the Commonwealth a part thereof, to be calculated on the proportion which his term of service with the State bears to his whole term of service, and for the purpose of the calculation his salary shall be taken to be that paid to him by the State at the time of the transfer.

Any officer who is, at the establishment of the Commonwealth, in the public service of a State, and who is, by consent of the Governor of the State with the advice of the Executive Council thereof, transferred to the public service of the Commonwealth, shall have the same rights as if he had been an officer of a department transferred to the Commonwealth and were retained in the service of the Commonwealth.

85. Transfer of property of State When any department of the public service of a State is transferred to the Commonwealth –

   (1.)   All property of the State of any kind, used exclusively in connexion with the department, shall become vested in the Commonwealth;

but, in the case of the departments controlling customs and excise and bounties, for such time only as the Governor-General in Council may declare to be necessary:

(2.) The Commonwealth may acquire any property of the State, of any kind used, but not exclusively used in connexion with the department; the value thereof shall, if no agreement can be made, be ascertained in, as nearly as may be, the manner in which the value of land, or of an interest in land, taken by the State for public purposes is ascertained under the law of the State in force at the establishment of the Commonwealth:

(3.) The Commonwealth shall compensate the State for the value of any property passing to the Commonwealth under this section; if no agreement can be made as to the mode of compensation, it shall be determined under laws to be made by the Parliament:

(4.) The Commonwealth shall, at the date of the transfer, assume the current obligations of the State in respect of the department transferred.

86. On the establishment of the Commonwealth, the collection and control of duties of customs and of excise, and the control of the payment of bounties, shall pass to the Executive Government of the Commonwealth.

87. During a period of ten years after the establishment of the Commonwealth and thereafter until the Parliament otherwise provides, of the net revenue of the Commonwealth from duties of customs and of excise not more than one-fourth shall be applied annually by the Commonwealth towards its expenditure.

The balance shall, in accordance with this Constitution, be paid to the several States, or applied towards the payment of interest on debts of the several States taken over by the Commonwealth.

88. Uniform duties of customs Uniform duties of customs shall be imposed within two years after the establishment of the Commonwealth.

89. Payment to States before uniform duties Until the imposition of uniform duties of customs –

(1.) The Commonwealth shall credit to each State the revenues collected therein by the Commonwealth.

(2.) The Commonwealth shall debit to each State –

(a) The expenditure therein of the Commonwealth incurred solely for the maintenance or continuance, as at the time of transfer, of any department transferred from the State to the Commonwealth;

(b) The proportion of the State, according to the number of its people, in the other expenditure of the Commonwealth.

(3.) The Commonwealth shall pay to each State month by month the balance (if any) in favour of the State.

90. Exclusive power over customs, excise, and bounties On the imposition of uniform duties of customs the power of the Parliament to impose duties of customs and of excise, and to grant bounties on the production or export of goods, shall become exclusive.

On the imposition of uniform duties of customs all laws of the several States imposing duties of customs or of excise, or offering bounties on the production or export of goods, shall cease to have effect, but any grant of or agreement for any such bounty lawfully made by or under the authority of the Government of any State shall be taken to be good if made before the thirtieth day of June, one thousand eight hundred and ninety-eight, and not otherwise.

91. Exceptions as to bounties Nothing in this Constitution prohibits a State from granting any aid to or bounty on mining for gold, silver, or other metals, nor from granting, with the consent of both Houses of the Parliament of the Commonwealth expressed by resolution, any aid to or bounty on the production or export of goods.

92. Trade within the Commonwealth to be free On the imposition of uniform duties of customs, trade, commerce, and intercourse among the States, whether by means of internal carriage or ocean navigation, shall be absolutely free.

But notwithstanding anything in this Constitution, goods imported before the imposition of uniform duties of customs into any State, or into any Colony which, whilst the goods remain therein, becomes a State, shall, on thence passing into another State within two years after the imposition of such duties, be liable to any duty chargeable on the importation of such goods into the Commonwealth, less any duty paid in respect of the goods on their importation.

93. Payment to States for five years after uniform tariffs During the first five years after the imposition of uniform duties of customs, and thereafter until the Parliament otherwise provides —

(1.) The duties of customs chargeable on goods imported into a State and afterwards passing into another State for consumption, and the duties of excise paid on goods produced or manufactured in a State and afterwards passing into another State for consumption, shall be taken to have been collected not in the former but in the latter State:

(2.) Subject to the last subsection, the Commonwealth shall credit revenue, debit expenditure, and pay balances to the several States as prescribed for the period preceding the imposition of uniform duties of customs.

94. Distribution of surplus After five years from the imposition of uniform duties of customs, the Parliament may provide, on such basis as it deems fair, for the monthly payment to the several States of all surplus revenue of the Commonwealth.

95. Customs duties of Western Australia Notwithstanding anything in this Constitution, the Parliament of the State of Western Australia, if that State be an Original State, may, during the first five years after the imposition of uniform duties of customs, impose duties of customs on goods passing into that State and not originally imported from beyond the limits of the Commonwealth; and such duties shall be collected by the Commonwealth.

But any duty so imposed on any goods shall not exceed during the first of such years the duty chargeable on the goods under the law of Western Australia in force at the imposition of uniform duties, and shall not exceed during the second, third, fourth, and fifth of such years respectively, four-fifths, three-fifths, two-fifths, and one-fifth of such latter duty, and all duties imposed under this section shall cease at the expiration of the fifth year after the imposition of uniform duties.

If at any time during the five years the duty on any goods under this section is higher than the duty imposed by the Commonwealth on the importation of the like goods, then such higher duty shall be collected on the goods when imported into Western Australia from beyond the limits of the Commonwealth.

96. Financial assistance to States During a period of ten years after the establishment of the Commonwealth and thereafter until the Parliament otherwise provides, the Parliament may grant financial assistance to any State on such terms and conditions as the Parliament thinks fit.

97. Audit Until the Parliament otherwise provides, the laws in force in any Colony which has become or becomes a State with respect to the receipt of revenue and the expenditure of money on account of the Government of the Colony, and the review and audit of such receipt and expenditure, shall apply to the receipt of revenue and the expenditure of money on account of the Commonwealth in the State in the same manner as if the Commonwealth, or the Government or an officer of the Commonwealth, were mentioned whenever the Colony, or the Government or an officer of the Colony, is mentioned.

98. Trade and commerce includes navigation and State railways The power of the Parliament to make laws with respect to trade and commerce extends to navigation and shipping, and to railways the property of any State.

99. Commonwealth not to give preference The Commonwealth shall not, by any law or regulation of trade, commerce, or revenue, give preference to one State or any part thereof over another State or any part thereof.

100. Nor abridge right to use water The Commonwealth shall not, by any law or regulation of trade or commerce, abridge the right of a State or of the residents therein to the reasonable use of the waters of rivers for conservation or irrigation.

101. Inter-State Commission There shall be an Inter-State Commission, with such powers of adjudication and administration as the Parliament deems necessary for the execution and maintenance, within the Commonwealth, of the provisions of this Constitution relating to trade and commerce, and of all laws made thereunder.

102. Parliament may forbid preferences by State The Parliament may by any law with respect to trade or commerce forbid, as to railways, any preference or discrimination by any State, or by any authority constituted under a State, if such preference or discrimination is undue and unreasonable, or unjust to any State; due regard being had to the financial responsibilities incurred by any State in connexion with the construction and maintenance of its railways. But no preference or discrimination shall, within the meaning of this section, be taken to be undue and unreasonable, or unjust to any State, unless so adjudged by the Inter-State Commission.

103. Commissioners' appointment, tenure, and remuneration The members of the Inter-State Commission —

    (1.)   Shall be appointed by the Governor-General in Council:

    (2.)   Shall hold office for seven years, but may be removed within that time by the Governor-General in Council, on an address from both Houses of the Parliament in the same session praying for such removal on the ground of proved misbehaviour or incapacity:

(3.)   Shall receive such remuneration as the Parliament may fix; but such remuneration shall not be diminished during their continuance in office.

104. Saving of certain rates Nothing in this Constitution shall render unlawful any rate for the carriage of goods upon a railway, the property of a State, if the rate is deemed by the Inter-State Commission to be necessary for the development of the territory of the State, and if the rate applies equally to goods within the State and to goods passing into the State from other States.

105. Taking over public debts of States [altered by No 3, 1910, s 2] The Parliament may take over from the States their public debts ~~as existing at the establishment of the Commonwealth~~, or a proportion thereof according to the respective numbers of their people as shown by the latest statistics of the Commonwealth, and may convert, renew, or consolidate such debts, or any part thereof; and the States shall indemnify the Commonwealth in respect of the debts taken over, and thereafter the interest payable in respect of the debts shall be deducted and retained from the portions of the surplus revenue of the Commonwealth payable to the several States, or if such surplus is insufficient, or if there is no surplus, then the deficiency or the whole amount shall be paid by the several States.

105A. Agreements with respect to State debts [inserted by No 1, 1929, s 2]–(1.) The Commonwealth may make agreements with the States with respect to the public debts of the States, including –

(*a*)   the taking over of such debts by the Commonwealth;

(*b*)   the management of such debts;

(*c*)   the payment of interest and the provision and management of sinking funds in respect of such debts;

(*d*)   the consolidation, renewal, conversion, and redemption of such debts;

(*e*)   the indemnification of the Commonwealth by the States in respect of debts taken over by the Commonwealth; and

(*f*)   the borrowing of money by the States or by the Commonwealth, or by the Commonwealth for the States.

(2.)   The Parliament may make laws for validating any such agreement made before the commencement of this section.

(3.)   The Parliament may make laws for the carrying out by the parties thereto of any such agreement.

(4.)   Any such agreement may be varied or rescinded by the parties thereto.

(5.)   Every such agreement and any such variation thereof shall be binding upon the Commonwealth and the States parties thereto notwithstanding anything contained in this Constitution or the Constitution of the several States or in any law of the Parliament of the Commonwealth or of any State.

(6.)   The powers conferred by this section shall not be construed as being limited in any way by the provisions of section one hundred and five of this Constitution.

CHAPTER 5.

THE STATES.

106. Saving of Constitutions The Constitution of each State of the Commonwealth shall, subject to this Constitution, continue as at the establishment of the Commonwealth, or as at the admission or establishment of the State, as the case may be, until altered in accordance with the Constitution of the State.

107. Saving of Power of State Parliaments Every power of the Parliament of a Colony which has become or becomes a State, shall, unless it is by this Constitution exclusively vested in the Parliament of the Commonwealth or withdrawn from the Parliament of the State, continue as at the establishment of the Commonwealth, or as at the admission or establishment of the State, as the case may be.

108. Saving of State laws Every law in force in a Colony which has become or becomes a State, and relating to any matter within the powers of the Parliament of the Commonwealth, shall, subject to this Constitution, continue in force in the State; and, until provision is made in that behalf by the Parliament of the Commonwealth, the Parliament of the State shall have such powers of alteration and of repeal in respect of any such law as the Parliament of the Colony had until the Colony became a State.

109. Inconsistency of laws When a law of a State is inconsistent with a law of the Commonwealth, the latter shall prevail, and the former shall, to the extent of the inconsistency, be invalid.

110. Provisions referring to Governor The provisions of this Constitution relating to the Governor of a State extend and apply to the Governor for the time being of the State, or other chief executive officer or administrator of the government of the State.

111. States may surrender territory The Parliament of a State may surrender any part of the State to the Commonwealth; and upon such surrender, and the acceptance thereof by the Commonwealth, such part of the State shall become subject to the exclusive jurisdiction of the Commonwealth.

112. States may levy charges for inspection laws After uniform duties of customs have been imposed, a State may levy on imports or exports, or on goods passing into or out of the State, such charges as may be necessary for executing the inspection laws of the State; but the net produce of all charges so levied shall be for the use of the Commonwealth; and any such inspection laws may be annulled by the Parliament of the Commonwealth.

113. Intoxicating liquids All fermented, distilled, or other intoxicating liquids passing into any State or remaining therein for use, consumption, sale, or storage, shall be subject to the laws of the State as if such liquids had been produced in the State.

114. States may not raise forces. Taxation of property of Commonwealth or State A State shall not, without the consent of the Parliament of the Commonwealth, raise or maintain any naval or military force, or impose any tax on property of any kind belonging to the Commonwealth, nor shall the Commonwealth impose any tax on property of any kind belonging to a State.

115. States not to coin money A State shall not coin money, nor make anything but gold and silver coin a legal tender in payment of debts.

116. Commonwealth not to legislate in respect of religion The Commonwealth shall not make any law for establishing any religion, or for imposing any religious observance, or for prohibiting the free exercise of any religion, and no religious test shall be required as a qualification for any office or public trust under the Commonwealth.

117. Rights of residents in States A subject of the Queen, resident in any State, shall not be subject in any other State to any disability or discrimination which would not be equally applicable to him if he were a subject of the Queen resident in such other State.

118. Recognition of laws, &c of States Full faith and credit shall be given, throughout the Commonwealth to the laws, the public Acts and records, and the judicial proceedings of every State.

119. Protection of States from invasion and violence The Commonwealth shall protect every State against invasion and, on the application of the Executive Government of the State, against domestic violence.

120. Custody of offenders against laws of the Commonwealth Every State shall make provision for the detention in its prisons of persons accused or convicted of offences against the laws of the Commonwealth, and for the punishment of persons convicted of such offences, and the Parliament of the Commonwealth may make laws to give effect to this provision.

CHAPTER 6.

NEW STATES.

121. New States may be admitted or established The Parliament may admit to the Commonwealth or establish new States, and may upon such admission or establishment make or impose such terms and conditions, including the extent of representation in either House of the Parliament, as it thinks fit.

122. Government of territories The Parliament may make laws for the government of any territory surrendered by any State to and accepted by the Commonwealth, or of any territory placed by the Queen under the authority of and accepted by the Commonwealth, or otherwise acquired by the Commonwealth, and may allow the representation of such territory in either House of the Parliament to the extent and on the terms which it thinks fit.

123. Alteration of limits of States The Parliament of the Commonwealth may, with the consent of the Parliament of a State, and the approval of the majority of the electors of the State voting upon the question, increase, diminish, or otherwise alter the limits of the State, upon such terms and conditions as may be agreed on, and may with the like consent, make provision respecting the effect and operation of any increase or diminution or alteration of territory in relation to any State affected.

124. Formation of new States A new State may be formed by separation of territory from a State, but only with the consent of the Parliament thereof, and a new State may be formed by the union of two or more States or parts of States, but only with the consent of the Parliaments of the States affected.

CHAPTER 7.

MISCELLANEOUS.

125. Seat of Government The seat of Government of the Commonwealth shall be determined by the Parliament, and shall be within territory which shall have been granted to or acquired by the Commonwealth, and shall be vested in and belong to the Commonwealth, and shall be in the State of New South Wales, and be distant not less than one hundred miles from Sydney.

Such territory shall contain an area of not less than one hundred square miles, and such portion thereof as shall consist of Crown lands shall be granted to the Commonwealth without any payment therefor.

The Parliament shall sit at Melbourne until it meet at the seat of Government.

126. Power to Her Majesty to authorise Governor-General to appoint deputies The Queen may authorise the Governor-General to appoint any person, or any persons jointly or severally, to be his deputy or deputies within any part of the Commonwealth, and in that capacity to exercise during the pleasure of the Governor-General such powers and functions of the Governor-General as he thinks fit to assign to such deputy or deputies, subject to any limitations expressed or directions given by the Queen; but the appointment of such deputy or deputies shall not affect the exercise by the Governor-General himself of any power or function.

127. [repealed by No 55, 1967, s 3]

CHAPTER 8.

ALTERATION OF THE CONSTITUTION.

128. Mode of altering the Constitution This Constitution shall not be altered except in the following manner: —

[this paragraph altered by No 84, 1977, s 2] The proposed law for the alteration thereof must be passed by an absolute majority of each House of the Parliament, and not less than two nor more than six months after its passage through both Houses the proposed law shall be submitted in each State **and Territory** to the electors qualified to vote for the election of members of the House of Representatives.

[this paragraph altered by No 84, 1977, s 2] But if either House passes any such proposed law by an absolute majority, and the other House rejects or fails to pass it, or passes it with any amendment to which the first- mentioned House will not agree, and if after an interval of three months the first-mentioned House in the same or the next session again passes the proposed law by an absolute majority with or without any amendment which has been made or agreed to by the other House, and such other House rejects or fails to pass it or passes it with any amendment to which the first-mentioned House will not agree, the Governor-General may submit the proposed law as last proposed by the first-mentioned House, and either with or without any amendments subsequently agreed to by both Houses, to the electors in each State **and Territory** qualified to vote for the election of the House of Representatives.

When a proposed law is submitted to the electors the vote shall be taken in such manner as the Parliament prescribes. But until the qualification of electors of members of the House of Representatives becomes uniform throughout the Commonwealth, only one-half the electors voting for and against the proposed law shall be counted in any State in which adult suffrage prevails.

And if in a majority of the States a majority of the electors voting approve the proposed law, and if a majority of all the electors voting also approve the proposed law, it shall be presented to the Governor-General for the Queen's assent.

No alteration diminishing the proportionate representation of any State in either House of the Parliament, or the minimum number of representatives of a State in the House of Representatives, or increasing, diminishing, or otherwise altering the limits of the State, or in any manner affecting the provisions of the Constitution in relation thereto, shall become law unless the majority of the electors voting in that State approve the proposed law.

[this paragraph added by No 84, 1977, s 2] In this section, "Territory" means any territory referred to in section one hundred and twenty-two of this Constitution in respect of which there is in force a law allowing its representation in the House of Representatives.

Index

Taxes and spending *continued*
    powers of House of Representatives and Senate, 50, 57, 90, 91
    redistributing revenue, 121
    States' taxing powers, 120, 121
    taxes must the same throughout Australia, 119
    tied grants, 123
    vertical fiscal imbalance, 121
    what Constitution says, 118
    where government gets its money, 118
    who taxes what, 120
Territories of Australia *see* Australian Territories
Trade between States, freedom of trade, 153
Treaties with other countries
    power of Australian government, 25
Trial by jury, 146
United Kingdom
    Australia becoming independent from, 22
    no single Constitution, 3, 144
United States
    Bill of Rights, 143
    Executive separate from Congress, 32
    model for Australian federal system, 112
Vertical fiscal imbalance, 121
Voting for Members of Parliament *see* Elections; Right to vote
Watchdogs, 103
Women
    not fully represented in Parliament
    right to vote, 29, 51